On the Track
of the
Poltergeist

By D. Scott Rogo

Anomalist Books
San Antonio • New York

To William G. Roll:
For his friendship, support and foreword

Contents

Part 3 APPENDIXES 185

Acknowledgments

Someone who investigates poltergeist cases rarely works alone. The investigations chronicled in this volume could not have been completed without a great deal of help and cooperation from some of my colleagues. Raymond Bayless deserves special credit for the help he has given me over the years as mentor and co-investigator on many of the cases reported here. Special thanks are also due to W. G. Roll and the Psychical Research Foundation in Chapel Hill, who have given me both moral and financial support over the years, especially in my undertaking of the Tucson case reported later in this book. Help on this difficult case was also given by Dr. Bruce Greyson, who helped to midwife the analysis of some of the psychological test data, and to the counseling center of the University of Arizona at Tucson for supplying me with much-needed material at very short notice. Dr. Gertrude Schmeidler of City College in New York was of immense assistance in the analysis of the Dell case recounted in Chapter 7. Both the UCLA Neuropsychiatric Institute and the Southern California Society for Psychical Research should be thanked for referring promising cases to me over the years.

Credit is also due to the many victims of poltergeists who

kindly invited me into their homes and cooperated in these investigations. It is only too bad that ensuring their privacy inhibits my ability to acknowledge their help openly. However, extra-special thanks are due to Mr. and Mrs. Richard Berkbigler of Tucson, Arizona, and their children for their wonderful cooperation, hospitality, and homemade tacos. Poltergeist investigations do tend to have a fair share of unexpected rewards!

Foreword

When I first met D. Scott Rogo some fifteen years ago, he was the *enfant terrible* of parapsychology—assertive, cocksure of himself, argumentative, a kind of poltergeist in the china shop of academic parapsychology. Perhaps this was because his training was different from that of most parapsychologists. Researchers usually come into the field through college or university training, after a great deal of research and sheltered under the wings of a prominent figure. Scott was self-taught. Where others read books to learn about parapsychology, Scott was writing them, and in the process he acquired a wide knowledge of the field. Though still a relatively young man, he has written more books in the field than any other living parapsychologist. And he is not an armchair author, since his books are enriched by his own investigations and researches.

The present volume contains some of his explorations into poltergeist and haunting cases. It also includes some of his ideas regarding the processes that animate these striking household disturbances. His studies illustrate the difficulty of excluding familiar physical explanations for these outbreaks, but they also illustrate the deep insights that can be gained into the processes

behind psychic phenomena once the researcher can satisfy himself that he is really dealing with psychokinesis or PK—the "mind
over matter" effect.

Usually poltergeist or RSPK (recurrent spontaneous PK)
outbreaks can be distinguished from haunting cases. The
source of the RSPK usually seems to be a current member of
the household while hauntings are generally held to be associated with a certain area, i.e., a "haunted house." Scott Rogo
makes the important point that there are also psychological reasons why people experience genuine ghosts and related
phenomena. But he also makes the further point that while
many poltergeist disturbances primarily stem from personal
problems the RSPK agent is undergoing, hauntings may be associated with more subtle, though no less real, family problems.
Scott goes on to give a balanced presentation of the two major
theories for the otogenesis of RSPK: the view that they are the
(paranormal) expression of hostility in the agent and the view
that they are due to neurological anomalies that erupt as psychic forces. He notes that the two theories may be complemen-
tary rather than contradictory, and also that some cases cannot
be simply explained by either.

This book also includes a good section on how to investigate cases and how to deal with the RSPK researcher's primary
dilemma—the family's need to bring the disturbances to a halt
and the researcher's need to have them continue so that they
may be observed under controlled conditions. Scott takes the
position that if the family wishes the incidents to cease, the researcher should help as best he can; for instance, by providing
couseling to reduce the psychological tensions that may be trig-
gering the incidents. Another route which I expect to hear
about in one of Scott's future books is bringing the occurrences
under conscious control. During our follow-up to the Tina
Resch "Columbus" poltergeist case recounted in Chapter 1, we
were able to reactivate the RSPK incidents in a non-destructive
and non-threatening way by means of hypnotic suggestion.
From having experienced the poltergeist as threatening and destructive (since it laid waste to the contents of her home), Tina
was able to direct her PK to special target objects of our own

choosing. Instead of something negative, she came to view her psychic ability as a special talent that she could use positively and that might asssist scientists in understanding the nature of psychic processes—and put them to use for the benefit of all mankind.

William G. Roll
Psychical Research Foundation
Chapel Hill, N.C.

Preface

There is no mystery greater than that posed by the poltergeist. The "noisy ghosts" of folklore and legend represent some of the most complex phenomena known to science.

   The book you are about to read is primarily an autobiographical account of my search to witness and document these rare phenomena. It also represents a critical reevaluation of what we know about the poltergeist. My feeling is that the poltergeist represents a much more formidable mystery than even many parapsychologists and scientists believe. Research undertaken both in this country and Europe since World War II indicates that poltergeists are not caused by spirits or demons but are creations released by the human mind. Psychological research indicates that poltergeists focus on unhappy families who tend to repress and sublimate massive amounts of their inner aggressions and anger. This anger tends to build within the unconscious mind of one of the family members until it explodes outward in the form of the poltergeist. This theory, called the "projected repression hypothesis," is the standard accepted explanation of the poltergeist and has been long honored by parapsychologists.

   But is it the whole answer?

The goal of this book is to show that it is not. By drawing on my own case material and investigations, I show that different poltergeist cases have different etiologies.

Apart from the study of the poltergeist, this book offers material on several cases that represent more typical "haunted houses." I have included these cases because they have often turned out to be caused by "hidden" or "camouflaged" poltergeists. These cases seem to fit in with the phenomenology of more traditional haunted houses. Detailed psychological research conducted with the families uncovered, however, that they themselves were actually psychically producing the phenomena. No ghosts nor outside agencies were the cause.

My second main purpose in writing this book is to present a kind of informal handbook on poltergeist hunting. Poltergeist cases crop up all the time, but the parapsychologist is usually the last person called in to investigate an outbreak. Police officers, fire officials, social service workers, electrical repairmen, and neighbors usually get consulted first! If *you* were to find yourself smack in the middle of an outbreak, how would *you* respond? The cases represented in this book represent a wide variety of poltergeist effects. Studying the strategies I used to deal with each of them will give you a good guide to how such cases should be handled. In order to sum up this material more systematically, some formal guidelines for conducting field investigations of this sort are contained in the concluding chapter.

Notice to the Reader

The following chapters chronicle several poltergeist investigations undertaken by me. The families involved never expected to find themselves in the limelight and tended to shy away from publicity. For this reason, the names of some of the witnesses have been changed to protect their privacy. Some peripheral identifying features of the cases have also been changed occasionally for this same reason. In two cases, the locations of the outbreaks have been altered to different parts of Los Angeles. In no way do these disguising features bear on the events themselves, which are faithfully recorded as reported or witnessed. The direct quotations contained within the accounts are not reconstructions, either, but are transcribed from tape recordings made by me during the course of my investigations. They have been corrected for grammatical accuracy or correct phaseology, however. None of the incidents has been sensationalized, and the true identities of the parties involved as well as the locations of the investigations remain on file. They may be inspected by qualified researchers.

1

Confronting the Poltergeist Mystery

"Ghosts" don't usually make nationwide headlines. But three times over the course of the past thirty years, papers across the continent have run headlines about suburban homes plagued by ghostly manifestations.

The first of these incidents dates back to 1958. The location was the residential community of Seaford, on Long Island in New York. Beginning that February, stories started appearing in the press about a series of strange episodes erupting in the home of Mr. and Mrs. James Herrmann and their four children. Knick-knacks were falling inexplicably from shelves, small objects were catapulting about, and even the household furniture was mysteriously overturning time and time again. Bottles kept in the refrigerator were particularly singled out by whatever force was loose in the house. Their caps would unscrew and even pop right off. The local police couldn't figure out what the cause was, nor was any high-frequency equipment operating in the area. (The experts who suggested this possibility never explained how such equipment could make bottle tops unscrew . . . but no matter.) No earth tremors were being recorded in the area either.

The first major clue to the nature of the disturbances came

only when two parapsychologists finally arrived on the scene from Duke University's parapsychology laboratory. The researchers set about studying the events and were able to make a series of fascinating discoveries. They noted first that the "force" liked to single out specific items in the house. In other words, certain household objects repeatedly moved by themselves. They also checked out the power inputs to the house to make sure that there were no power surges coming into the residence. But their most significant discovery was that the events were focusing on one of the family's children. They usually occurred only when twelve-year-old Jimmy Herrmann was up and about, and they abated when he was away from the house. Despite the natural suspicions aroused by this discovery, the boy refused to confess that he was manufacturing the incidents. These claims to innocence were later substantiated when the ghostly disturbances broke out even when his every movement in the house was carefully monitored. The disturbances, however, gradually ceased, and the Herrmanns were able to live in the house for several more years without incident.

The same sort of activity hit the media again on November 25, 1974. Now the wire services across the United States began carrying stories about the weird activities going on in a small house located in Bridgeport, Connecticut. The fantastic reports told of household items flying about, silverware shooting around like guided missiles, and a rambunctious television set that kept hopping off its stand. The chief witnesses and victims of this eerie drama were Mr. and Mrs. Gerald Goodin and their children. By the end of the week, both the clergy and the police were at the scene of the action, eager to find a solution to the mystery. Hundreds of spectators started showing up on the front lawn of the house in hopes of witnessing the events.

The onlookers began to leave when the police reported shortly thereafter that they had solved the mystery. The *Los Angeles Times*, for instance, carried a report that ". . . the unusual happenings witnessed by police and firemen in a private home were a hoax perpetrated by a 10-year-old girl." It seems that Meredith Goodin, the couple's adopted daughter, "admitted tossing around furniture when no one was looking."

The problem with this solution was, frankly, that no one personally involved with the case believed it even for a second!

It turned out that the police, totally unable to come up with a solution to the disturbances, eventually turned their frustrations on the poor girl as their last resort. They then badgered her into a confession. Besides causing a lot of hard feeling, this tactic did little to quell either the disturbances or the continuing testimony of the primary witnesses . . . including some of the police investigators themselves, many of whom publicly criticized the report. The first officer to answer the Goodin's frantic call, John Holsworth, told reporters that the events he witnessed couldn't have been faked. "I saw the heavy refrigerator lift slowly off the floor," he claimed. "There was no one else around. Then the big TV set seemed to float in the air and crash to the floor."

Needless to say, Bridgeport's police officials never explained how a preteenaged girl could hoist a refrigerator in the air without being seen doing it by anyone in the room. Another officer who arrived on the scene that day told reporters, "I just couldn't believe what I saw. Shelves fixed to the walls began to vibrate until they broke loose, then flew through the air."

Despite this kind of testimony, the police made a hasty exit from the case after releasing their explanation to the press. The Goodins were left with no alternative but to move elsewhere.

Probably the most recent case of this sort is still in the public's mind, since on this occasion one of the incidents was actually photographed. Columbus, Ohio was the scene of all the action, which focused on the home of Mr. and Mrs. John Resch, their son, their foster children, and their adopted daughter. The activity began on March 3, 1984, when the lights in the house began turning off and on. Then the television and radio settings started acting up in similar fashion. When knickknacks and furniture commenced toppling over or flying about, the family realized that they needed help. Their first suspicion was that some sort of power malfunction was causing the inconvenience, but the electrician who came to check it out left the house more puzzled than when he arrived. Bruce Claggett, the repairman, later explained to the press that the lights had kept turning themselves on during his visit to the house. He testified that he personally taped down the switches on several occasions, only to see the lights turn back on as soon as his back was turned. The Resch's five foster children were playing in the den at the time, so they couldn't have been responsible. Mr. and Mrs. Resch went out later that night, leaving Claggett home with Tina, their adopted daughter. Claggett and Tina then taped down all the downstairs switches, but every time they left a particular room, the lights would suddenly come on. This phenomenon occurred several times while Tina remained in the repairman's direct presence. The bewildered man only reluctantly entertained the thought that something supernatural was going on.

The Resch family realized they were up against a psychic adversary only when the occurrences began focusing directly on their adopted fifteen-year-old daughter. So, having explored technology and science for a solution to their growing problem, the Resches turned to religion. Their son was a Mormon convert, and he lost little time inviting some church members to the house. They prayed and tried to drive out the infesting entity, but the rites seemed to irritate rather than exorcise the invader.

With no other solution in sight, the Resches finally appealed to the press. That's how the *Columbus Dispatch,* which first publicized the story, became involved in the case. When their own reporters witnessed the activity and even photographed a telephone flying through the air, they suggested to Mrs. Resch that she call in a parapsychologist.

The most impressive testimony came from Fred Shannon, one of the *Dispatch's* photographers. He watched the two living room phones literally catapult across the room on several occasions. He also saw two candlesticks slide across a table, accompanied by a horrendous noise like a locomotive! But his most curious experience came when he saw a Kleenex box in the living room jet about from one table to another. Shannon personally told me in August 1984 that the box did not bounce when it landed, but instantly *stuck* to the table as though landing on super-glue. This, more than any other incident, proved to him that the events were paranormal.

Mrs. Resch could see no relief in sight, so she finally agreed to the newspaper's suggestion and contacted W. G. Roll, project director of the Psychical Research Foundation in Chapel Hill, North Carolina. This was a singularly good choice, since Roll has made a virtual career out of studying such outbreaks. Roll, who is probably one of the friendliest researchers in the field, is Danish by birth. By education he is British, but he has been living in the United States for over three decades. Although he began his parapsychological career at Oxford University as an experimentalist, his interest soon began focusing on poltergeist investigations and the complex issue of life after death. He pursued these interests after he joined the staff of the Duke University parapsychology laboratory in the 1950s. When he investigated his first major case in 1958, he got bitten by the poltergeist bug, and to this day he is one of this country's leading authorities on the subject.

Roll, who spent a week at the Resches' house, has only recently finished up his investigation and report on the case. When I was able to track him down in Atlanta to talk to him about the case, he admitted that he had directly witnessed some of the poltergeist phenomena. (This was no surprise since he had already made similar statements to the press.) He told me that although the poltergeist beat a hasty retreat when he and his assistant first arrived on the scene, it made a noisy comeback by the end of the week. The most impressive series of incidents occurred on Thursday, March 15, when he was personally able to witness a brief flurry of activity. The most imposing incidents, he explained, occurred when he and Tina were alone on the upper floor of the house. They had gone there only moments before, after hearing some objects being thrown about.

"Things began happening upstairs," he explained, "so I got very close to Tina and was with her for a period of time up there. I had my tape recorder on to keep a running account of what took place. Something fell in the bathroom [adjoining the master bedroom], I think it was a bar of soap, and we walked into the bathroom from the bedroom. Then as we walked out of the bathroom and passed by the door, a picture on the wall to our left fell to the floor. It was right next to us, and we saw it fall to the ground."

Roll went on to say that Tina became upset by the incident,

since the picture was one of her mother's favorites. Luckily it wasn't broken, even though it had ripped the nail holding it from the wall. The ever-optimistic investigator merely suggested that they nail it back up again and even volunteered to tackle the chore. That's when the poltergeist started acting up again.

"I was keeping Tina under close watch throughout this period," said Roll. "So when I hammered in the nail, she was standing right next to me, and I was very aware of her exact position and what she was doing—which was just watching what I was doing. Before I proceeded, I placed my tape recorder on the dresser, which was behind us and to our left. As I was hammering in the nail we heard a sound like something falling to the floor. We turned around and found that my tape recorder was on the ground."

The machine had moved about nine feet from its original position, and Roll could see no way that Tina could have so much as touched it. But he was in for more surprises.

"I had been putting the nail in the wall with a pair of pliers I had found on the dresser," he continued, "and I put them back down where the recorder had been. We were examining the tape recorder when there was a sound from the other side of the room. When we examined that area, we found the pair of pliers lying on the floor behind the bed. They had moved five or six feet from their position on the dresser."

Of course, cries of fraud and hoax were soon being made about the case. Three representatives from the Buffalo-based Committee for the Scientific Investigation of Claims of the Paranormal showed up at the Resch home on March 13 while Roll was still undertaking his investigation. Included on the team was the rather notorious James "the Amazing" Randi from Runsum, New Jersey, who was already publicly criticizing the case. The CSICOP investigators became even more skeptical when the Resches refused to allow the debunker into the house. The Resches didn't object to the other men, who were both scientists, but they put their foot down about Randi. The entire team decided to withdraw and subsequently issued several negative statements about the case.

"We've had a circus. Now we have a magic show. No. Not

here," was Mrs. Resch's response to the press about the incident.

However, the most serious allegations of fraud came when several news reporters saw and filmed Tina deliberately knocking over a lamp. Oddly, though, even they tended to discount the incident in light of the impressive evidence already backing the case. Mrs. Resch later explained that Tina was virtually being held a captive in the house by the sensation-seeking reporters. The teenager threw the lamp just so they would be satisfied and then go away.

Roll, however, feels that some additional but limited fraud was probably involved. "It is certain that Tina threw a lamp down on one occasion," he said. "That's obvious. She told me that she did the same thing on two other occasions. So there's no doubt that there were some fraudulent occurrences."

Nevertheless, Roll was not daunted by the fact that some fraud took place. It is typical for children in poltergeist-ridden homes to get into the act by engaging in just this sort of mischief-making. The occurrence of occasional fraud does not necessarily ruin the value of many otherwise impressive outbreaks. "I can only say," cautioned the researcher, "that when I was present, I couldn't find any ordinary explanation for the incidents I witnessed. In my opinion, it is very unlikely that they were caused normally. And of course, there were a number of other witnesses we interviewed in Columbus who had seen things under conditions where no family members could have caused them."

To complete the investigation, Roll took Tina back to North Carolina with him later that month, where he and other parapsychologists conducted several computer-based ESP and PK tests with her. The results of these experiments had not been thoroughly analyzed at the time I spoke with Roll, but the researcher did explain that "nothing very striking" occurred during them. The trip to North Carolina also gave Tina a respite from the limelight, and at Roll's suggestion she underwent counseling to deal better with the ordeal she was facing. Since Tina stayed in Roll's home in Durham, her visit enabled the researcher to observe some of her poltergeistery at even closer quarters.

"There were some PK (psychokinetic) incidents in my home and at the home of one of the counselors," Roll admitted. He was most impressed by one specific display of object-throwing that occurred in his presence.

"Again I had close watch over Tina," he explained. "She was about five or six feet away from me and there was a small table behind her and to the right. There was a candlestick and candle on the table, and as I was talking to her, there was a crashing sound behind her. The candle had moved out of the candle holder about nine feet, hitting the wall behind her. The table was in my view but I didn't see the candle take off. The movement appeared to be very fast."

Roll also noted that Tina was not in physical contact with the table and had made no suspicious movements directly before the incident.

"There was no way she could have caused the event normally," Roll admitted.

I also learned that several incidents had occurred in the home of Tina's psychologist. The psychologist testified that a door flew open by itself when Tina was standing in front of her, and knocked the girl over. When they were hugging at the end of one session, the psychologist also saw a pencil fly off a table and hurl itself across the room. This incident was especially impressive since Tina was being physically restrained (in a positive sense!) at the time.

The three accounts you have just read are representative of several that have been reported within recent years. Similar stories have emanated from just about every country in the world. The technical name for such a disturbance is a *poltergeist*, a German word that roughly translates as "noisy ghost." Poltergeists, however, are very different from your more traditional ghost, since wispy and ephemeral phantoms are practically never seen during these outbreaks. Poltergeists delight, instead, in throwing furniture about violently, creating pounding noises, setting fires, causing rocks to rain down on the homes they are attacking, and so on. These attacks tend to be brief and rarely last for more than a few weeks or months before dying out completely. It is also important to note that they are not particularly linked to the houses they attack but seem more interested in the families living there. If a family besieged by the poltergeist flees to a new residence, the commotion is very likely to follow.

Probably the most notable characteristic of the poltergeist, however, is that it tends to focus on a specific person living in the house. If that person leaves to take a vacation or go to school, the poltergeistery will usually stop until he or she returns. The same pattern holds true should the focus person go to sleep.

This pattern was certainly true of the three cases that opened this chapter. The Seaford poltergeist revolved around twelve-year-old Jimmy Herrmann, whereas both the Bridgeport and Columbus cases focused their activity on adopted youngsters living with the key families. Note that all of these poltergeist foci were rather young.

Parapsychologists have, in fact, known for years that poltergeists particularly focus on children. This pattern was first recognized as far back as the 1890s. Of course, many of the first parapsychologists merely believed that the outbreaks were pranks perpetrated by these youngsters. Perhaps this was a logical if myopic conclusion to reach. But since that time, dozens of poltergeist displays have been investigated and even witnessed with positive results by parapsychologists. So we definitely know that these children are at least not normally responsible for the attacks. It also seems obvious that they somehow hold the clue to the nature of these mysterious outbreaks. So let's look at these poltergeist children in a little more depth. Just who are they?

Well, to begin with, they tend to be young. Of some 116 poltergeist cases reported in detail from the seventeenth century to the present, about two-thirds have involved adolescents. Only 18 cases involved adults. The average age of the children in these reports is thirteen. It also appears that, at least today, just as many boys as girls become poltergeist victims.

Statistics are fine as far as they go, but they do little to help us understand just *why* certain children become poltergeist victims. Poltergeists tend to be rare occurrences, so what makes these children unique? Why do only a few individuals end up as poltergeist victims?

There seems to be one primary clue in answer to these nagging questions. This clue rests within the psychology of the individual child. But to understand this clue, we'll have to transport ourselves back in time by about twenty years.

Parapsychology's first real breakthrough in the study and understanding of the poltergeist came in 1967. It was the result of a case that broke out in Miami, Florida. This poltergeist was holding forth in the warehouse of a novelty company, where it was spending most of its time making specialty items (carefully placed on tiered shelves) fling themselves across the storeroom or to the floor. The activity was going on day and night, and many witnesses were able to observe the displays. The intensity of the case was severe. W. G. Roll, now in charge of his own parapsychology organization in Durham, lost little time getting down to Florida as soon as he learned about the case. It didn't take him long to determine that the breakage focused on a nineteen-year-old Cuban refugee, Julio Vasquez, who was working in the warehouse. By studying the general pattern of the events, Roll was also able to make another crucial discovery. The poltergeist was prone to break out whenever the young man was particularly upset or tense. The frustrated and uptight teenager was even partially aware of this pattern himself . . . and his own inexplicable complicity in the case.

This factor became more obvious as events progressed. Julio even told one witness that whenever one of the novelty items fell and broke, "I feel happy; that thing [the breakage] makes me happy; I don't know why."

Observations and comments such as these served as obvious clues about the nature of the disturbances. So Roll took Julio back with him to North Carolina, where two psychologists were asked to examine him. Their conclusions were startling. Both psychologists determined that Julio was hardly the carefree young man he appeared to be. Detailed psychological tests and interviews led the clinicians to conclude that their subject was rather disturbed. They found that he was harboring intense feelings of guilt and rejection, yet he displayed a crippling inability to express these feelings in a socially acceptable way. Instead he tried to deny or shrink from displaying any overt hostility in his private life. The psychologists came to view Julio's unconscious mind as a hot-bed of repressed hostility ready to blow at any moment. These inner conflicts were especially directed toward his stepmother, with whom he was living. They had then carried over to his employer.

Psychological dynamics such as these actually "explain" the core nature of the poltergeist rather well. Parapsychologists currently believe that these "noisy ghosts" are actually psychologically generated phenomena. Roll, for instance, doesn't even like to use the term *poltergeist,* since it implies that such disturbances are caused by some sort of entity or ghost. He has renamed the phenomenon "recurrent spontaneous psychokinesis," or RSPK for short. He believes, like most other researchers, that poltergeist eruptions occur when unconscious frustration—normally barred from consciousness—builds in the agent's mind until it can't be contained any longer. What results is a huge psychic explosion that unleashes the poltergeist. The poltergeist is, therefore, both an expression and a release mechanism (or safety valve) of and for this inner hostility.

This explanation also tells us a great deal about the specific dynamics of the poltergeist—that is, it actually explains quite neatly just *why* the poltergeist acts the way it does. I am sure that all readers of this book have seen what happens when a young child becomes frustrated, or when one becomes angry after being scolded for being naughty. The child is apt to throw a tantrum by slamming doors, throwing toys about, banging on the walls, and displaying other aggressive acts. It doesn't take much insight to realize that these are the exact activities in which the poltergeist engages. Like a frustrated youngster, it too bangs on the walls, throws things, and slams doors.

This theory may sound rather far-fetched. But in the years since 1967, several poltergeist children have been psychologically examined and tested. The same consistent factors tend to emerge in case after case. This is not only true of the cases Roll investigated, but other researchers have begun isolating a similar syndrome. Chief among these independent researchers has been Dr. Hans Bender of the Institute for the Study of Border Areas of Psychology in Freiburg, Germany.

Bender encountered one of his most challenging cases when a rather bizarre poltergeist began rampaging about in the small town of Nickleheim. This poltergeist attack lasted for four months during 1968–1969, plaguing the home of a blue-collar worker, his wife, and their thirteen-year-old daughter, Brigitte. The poltergeist had begun its antics by banging on the door of the house at all hours. Later, rocks began mysteriously pelting down on the roof as though falling out of the sky. (This is, by the way, one of the poltergeist's favorite tricks, and I will recount my own firsthand experience with such a case later in this book.) Household furniture began to move about eerily soon after the rock-throwing episodes. Eventually the family called in a priest to exorcise the place, but the ritual did little good. In fact, it seems that at the very moment the priest blessed the house, a stone came falling from the ceiling. When it struck the floor, it didn't bounce as it normally should have. It remained glued in place, as though fastened by a magnet. The priest picked it up and found that it was inexplicably warm.

No one knew just how the rock could have gotten into the house. It apparently just materialized out of thin air, or had been somehow mysteriously transferred into the room through a solid wall.

This trick, popularly called *teleportation,* eventually became one of the Nickleheim poltergeist's trademarks. One of the witnesses to the poltergeist, who had aided Bender in an earlier investigation, deliberately tried to prompt the "geist" into showing off its teleporting powers under controlled conditions. As Bender writes in his official report on the case:

> He put bottles containing perfume and tablets on the kitchen table, asked the inhabitants of the house to go outside, closed all the windows and doors, and then left himself. After a short time, the perfume bottle appeared in the air outside the house, and a bit later on, the bottle of tablets appeared in the air at the height of the roof and fell to the ground in a zigzag manner.

I might add that this unusual zigzag movement has been reported in many poltergeist cases. Objects thrown by the poltergeist often do not follow normal trajectories. They will frequently move unusually slowly as though floating or being deliberately carried, will sometimes make right-angle turns in midflight, and have been known to fly at incredible speeds and then just stop in midair and fall to the ground.

Bender personally witnessed one of these peculiar teleportations one night while visiting the family. It was a cold winter's evening, and he had just arrived and hung his coat on a rack. Only a few brief moments later he discovered that the coat was missing. It was immediately found *outside* the house, several feet away from the building, laid out and neatly folded on a bed of snow. There wasn't so much as one footprint around it! The entire family had been with Bender at the time, and the incident apparently transpired in the twinkling of an eye.

The Nickleheim poltergeist gradually petered out, but not before Bender was able to clinically evaluate thirteen-year-old Brigitte, around whom the poltergeist was focusing. He found that she was having a difficult time dealing with her own rapidly evolving sexual maturation, and that sexual preoccupations were stirring up a hornet's nest of repressed conflicts.

Bender has, in fact, been able to clinically evaluate several poltergeist agents since that time and has concluded that they all have basically unstable personalities. He found them impulsive with no tolerance for frustration, and possessed with a curious tendancy to "displace" or "deny" their feelings of hostility. Note how similar these patterns are to the psychological characteristics that Roll has discovered among his American poltergeist counterparts.

None of this means, however, that repressed hostility represents the total solution to the poltergeist mystery. Even Roll himself, who did so much to pioneer the repressed-hostility theory, has never claimed that psychological factors taken alone represent the entire answer to the question. It serves merely as the setting from which the poltergeist emerges . . . and little more.

At the present time, in fact, parapsychologists are still grappling with two major mysteries posed by the poltergeist. We'll examine each in turn.

Where Does the Poltergeist Get Its Energy?

Even though we know the psychological causes of the poltergeist, we still have no idea *how* it carries out its stunning displays. Generally though, three theories have been proposed over the years that can possibly explain the poltergeist's varied mechanisms.

On the basis of the several cases that Roll has personally investigated, he has come to the conclusion that the typical poltergeist is somehow created by a force housed in the brain and body of the agent himself. He came to this conclusion after making some peculiar discoveries about how the psychokinetic phenomena of poltergeists seem to function. Basing his views on several detailed analyses, he has been able to show that objects in close physical proximity to the probable agent will move more often than distant ones. The more distant objects, however, tend to travel longer distances and in the opposite direction than do "close proximity" objects. These findings indicated to Roll that the poltergeist force probably emanates from two places on the agent's body that take on the function of "rotating beams" of force. These beams then spin around the agent's body, flinging about any objects with which they come into contact.

Unfortunately such findings do not appear to be universal. Dr. Hans Bender, for example, has been a rather open critic of Roll's theories because he has been unable to confirm them on the basis of his own case studies. He suggests instead that the poltergeist agent does not actually project a force from his body or mind *per se*, but merely acts as a center that collects and redirects normal sources of energy. For instance, our air is full of free-floating energy. If you were to lower the temperature of an average-size room just one degree, a tremendous amount of energy would be conserved. It is Bender's view that somehow the poltergeist agent psychically draws energy from these random sources, reorders it, and redirects it into producing the weird antics of the poltergeist.

A third theory about the mechanics of the poltergeist was suggested several years ago by Dr. Nandor Fodor, a Hungarian psychoanalyst who was also an avid poltergeist hunter. His ideas are a little more speculative than either Roll's or Bender's. He suggested that a poltergeist agent might be suffering from some sort of "psychic lobotomy"—that is, the poltergeist may be masterminded by some portion of the agent's unconscious mind that has physically detached itself from its host's brain, psyche, and body, and has developed a primitive intelligence of its own. Fodor was therefore one of the few parapsychologists to argue that the poltergeist is generated by some sort of intelligent entity somewhat independent of the agent's own will. He believed that somehow this split-off portion of the mind controls some sort of energy or force that it could use to produce poltergeist displays.

What Are the Physiological Conditions under which the Poltergeist Erupts?

Speaking before a meeting of parapsychologists held in 1983 at Fairleigh Dickinson University (in Madison, New Jersey), Roll stated that purely psychological factors represent ". . . only one-half of the solution to the poltergeist mystery." But just what *is* the other half?

In the middle of the 1970s, Roll and his colleagues began thinking in terms of neurology. He began his serious study of this possibility in February 1975 when a very frightened family, living in a small (undisclosed) town in Michigan, contacted him. Roll called them the "Muellers" in his official report. The family consisted of Mr. and Mrs. Mueller and their two sons, aged nineteen and twenty-one. The events seemed to be focusing on the older son, Peter, who was suffering from epilepsy. The first manifestations had actually begun in July 1974 and consisted of violent poundings on the walls of the house. The noises would come in short bursts of activity, and the family's first response was to call the police. The noises recurred every night for two months, except for two short periods in September. The police made eight visits to the house but could find no explanation for the disturbances. But when the older son was sent to the hospital in October for some medical treatments, the noises ceased until his return. Several neighbors witnessed the events at about this time, which now sounded more like explosions than poundings. One of the "raps" was so powerful that it cracked the kitchen ceiling!

The phenomena began accelerating in December when lamps, pillows, and other objects in the house proceeded to fly about. Fires erupted mysteriously as the poltergeist reached its zenith.

Even though the family was aware that Peter was the focal point of the problem, the true nature of his involvement wasn't discerned until Gerald Solfvin and W. G. Roll from the Psychical Research Foundation investigated the case. They found that the poltergeist activity was directly related to certain aspects of the young man's medical history—and especially to his epilepsy.

Peter's epilepsy had been first diagnosed in March 1974, but his major convulsions began in September of that year . . . during the very week the poltergeist went into its momentary abeyance. The beginnings of the poundings also were traceable to the time of the first major medical problems that led to Peter being diagnosed as epileptic. These clues were just too consistent for Solfvin and Roll to dismiss as coincidental, and they led Roll to suggest that they were critical to the psychokinesis. He felt that the propensity for Peter's brain to produce storms of neuronal activity was somehow also unleashing the psychokinetic storms comprising the poltergeist. Psychological stress and frustration would then have been the complicating factor timing the outbreaks. He later wrote about this and similar cases that ". . . in many respects, the classic poltergeist agent begins to look like an ideopathic epileptic whose massive discharges in the brain are now somehow transformed into RSPK."

With these new discoveries and clinical data at hand, Roll next decided to recheck the data he had collected from several earlier investigations. He had made it standard procedure to take brain wave recordings from the agents in those cases. By reexamining this data, the parapsychologist found suspicious evidence of epileptic-like patterns in their clinical EEGs as well. The indications were more subtle, though.

These findings and data do not necessarily prove that a relationship exists between epilepsy and poltergeists. But the possibility remains that these psychic storms emerge from a conglomeration of personal, mental, and neurological factors.

Probably the most important issue at stake, however, is what the poltergeist is telling us about humans and their minds: The existence of the poltergeist should be serving as a warning to us. It is all too easy in this Aquarian Age of ours to extol the virtues of the human mind and its potentials for psychic and spiritual growth. But the existence of the poltergeist indicates that these powers can be destructive as well as beneficial. This unwelcomed destructive power represents the dark side of the mind. If we wish to develop and use our inner psychic potentials, we will first have to learn to tame them. The existence of the poltergeist indicates that we have so far failed.

In the chapters that follow, I will be describing my own encounters with the poltergeist. Over the years these encounters have alerted me to even more clues about the nature of these disturbances.

My own experiences have been less stereotyped than those reported by Roll or Bender, who have specialized in the "disturbed adolescent" variety of poltergeist activity. So my observations and views about the poltergeist have tended to go in different directions from their work and theories. Some of my personal experiences support their viewpoints and ideas, while other observations I have been able to make do not. The following case studies and investigations tend to indicate that the poltergeist is a multifaceted phenomenon; one that can be catalyzed by a great many factors above and beyond simple repressed hostility. These factors might be working singly or in conjunction with others in any given case. Does this mean, then, that my research contradicts those of other researchers? No, it doesn't. For in the long run, we know relatively little about the specific psychology or physics of the poltergeist. The research I have carried out—like that of Roll and Bender, as well as many others—should be viewed as individual pieces of a huge jigsaw puzzle that parapsychologists are trying to put together. Gradually a specific picture of the poltergeist will begin taking shape as our researches proceed.

Perhaps the situation has been best summarized by Dr. John Beloff of the University of Edinburgh, who is one of Great Britain's most eminent parapsychologists. He recently observed that we hardly know more about the poltergeist today than we did two hundred years ago, when spirits or demons were blamed for these disturbances. This statement is, of course, a gross exaggeration; but it aptly reflects how much more we will need to know before we can claim that science has solved the mystery of the poltergeist.

Part 1

Four Major Investigations

2
A Poltergeist in Los Angeles

"Hello, Scott? Quick! Write down this address."

These were the words with which Raymond Bayless greeted me when I picked up the phone at 4:45 P.M. on October 9, 1974. His next words were even more urgent. "I think we may have a live one," he pressed.

In parapsychology lingo, a "live one" usually designates a hot case, such as a haunting or poltergeist, that is still going strong. Raymond didn't have to tell me more; he was on to a promising case; one that was probably still picking up steam and ripe for an on-the-spot investigation. Raymond's message signified that time was of the essence.

After giving me the address of the house where the activity was currently erupting, Raymond filled me in on the background.

The case first came to light when a Mrs. Edna Downs started calling television station KTLA in Los Angeles. She had been calling all week, complaining that objects were flying around her house and that a mysterious prowler was pounding on her front door. She had called the police the first night of the nuisance, but they were unable to find the "culprit" responsible. The poundings even battered in the front screen door, and the police were at least taking her story seriously. Since the police couldn't find the culprit, Mrs. Downs was in more of a dilemna than ever . . . especially when small pieces of furniture in the house started toppling over. Small household objects mysteriously catapulted from shelves and tables as well. Her only conclusion was that a demon was loose in the house, which prompted her to call some Catholic priests in the local community. But they had merely laughed at her. With no other recourse in sight, Mrs. Downs had finally begun calling the television station. The news department really didn't know what to make of the woman's story, and the assignment editor finally called up the office of the Southern California Society for Psychical Research in hopes that perhaps they could shed some light on the mystery. That's how the case came to Raymond's attention.

Raymond happened to be in the Society's office at the time, so the call was turned over to him. The assignment editor from KTLA was at first reluctant to give him any specific details about the case, but Raymond finally succeeded in getting the name, address, and phone number of the family involved. He called them immediately and learned that the case was not only still active, but "acting up" raucously. Not only were household objects flying around in a dizzying array of poltergeistery, but they were even hitting people! Raymond explained to the frightened and bewildered family that he was quite familiar with their problem and asked if he might visit them. They consented, which prompted Raymond to call me because we often coinvestigate promising cases.

I dashed for my tape recorder and sport coat as soon as I hung up the phone. I didn't want to lose any time getting to the house, since any delay might cause me to miss observing the action for myself. Throwing on my coat and tie, I bolted for my car, silently praying all the while that I could avoid rush hour traffic while trying to get downtown where the house was located.

I was lucky. I was able to make the drive into Los Angeles in about half an hour, and I arrived at the address Raymond had given me at 5:30 P.M. The house was situated in an old middle-class section of town, and it was a rather rundown two-story building. It was only later that I realized that it was actually a duplex, and that part of the downstairs area was partitioned off into a separate dwelling. The scene of the poltergeist was in the main structure, which took up half of the downstairs area and all of the upstairs, which extended over the other unit.

I've been investigating ghosts and poltergeists for many years, but never have I seen so odd a sight as I did that October day. A white-haired elderly woman was sitting on the porch with a stunningly attractive teenage girl sitting beside her. At first glance the girl struck me as a very mature—in every respect— seventeen-year-old. I assumed that these were the distressed residents of the house, and my impression was confirmed when they both got up to greet me. After I introduced myself, they pointed to a middle-aged woman sitting in a nearby car feeding a baby. The elderly woman explained that she, too, lived in the house but had been driven out by the "demon." A quick conversation revealed that the house did not, in fact, belong to Mrs. Downs, with whom I was speaking and who had originally called KTLA. The permanent occupants were really her daughter, Mrs. Katherine James, and Mrs. James's own daughter Chris.* I was rather surprised to learn that Chris was only thirteen years old, since she looked and acted so much more mature.

I made all these connections during the course of a brief and very confused conversation I held with the family within moments of my arrival. All of them were very frightened, and seemed very relieved that I was there. Soon they were all talking at once, trying to fill me in on what was happening.

I felt that my first responsibility was to calm the family down, carefully but firmly. I knew from my experience that poltergeist attacks follow rather conventional patterns and rarely hurt anybody. I wasn't being too presumptuous, therefore, when I assured the family that no one would be hurt by whatever "force" was plaguing them. (I didn't want to further worry them by hinting or even implying that spirits or demons might be at

---

*In several earlier summaries of this case, I refer to Mrs. Downs as Chris's aunt. This change was made in order to protect the identity of the family. Since the case is now ten years old, there seems little reason to alter any of the circumstances, which is why this account will differ in some respects from my other writings on it.

the root of the disturbance.) I tried to demythologize the occurrences by stating that I knew of many families who had found
themselves up against similar problems and that I would try to
help them through it. I explained that there was little likelihood
that spirits or demons had anything to do with the disturbance,
but that some more impersonal force was causing the problem.
I especially assured Mrs. Downs and Mrs. James that such infestations can be nerve-shattering, but not really dangerous.

The frenzy that first greeted me turned into a few nervous
smiles as I urged the family to return to the house. They seemed
to have some misgivings. Finally, Chris reluctantly offered to
escort me into the building, but Mrs. James still refused to go
since—despite my assurances—she was still frightened that her
baby would be hurt. Because the front door was locked from the
inside (apparently by the poltergeist), Mrs. Downs and Chris took
me through the kitchen door at the rear of the house. Our brief
walk resembled a guided tour of a battle zone as Mrs. Downs and
Chris showed me a battered screen door and, once we were
inside the house, all sorts of broken knickknacks lying about.
Fingernail polish was splashed over the walls, small lotion bottles
were lying incongruously here and there, and broken glass pep-
pered the kitchen. The "evil spirit" that was plaguing the house
was blamed for all the mess. Our little tour continued as Chris
took me through the central hallway to the living room, while
Mrs. Downs stayed behind to clean up in the kitchen.

My introduction to the poltergeist came at that moment.
When I first stepped into the living room, my attention was drawn
to the open stairwell that led to the upstairs bedrooms and bathroom. No sooner had I entered the living room than I heard a
curious "pop" as though something had been thrown against a
wall upstairs. Chris and I shot each other knowing glances.

"Does the phenomenon ever make rapping noises?" I
asked.

"Yes, it's throwing things," she answered nervously.

I scurried upstairs to look around, hopefully to retrieve
whatever had been thrown. The stairs ended on a landing that led
to bedrooms on the left and right, and to a bathroom directly to
the front, but displaced slightly to the left. I certainly couldn't tell

if anything had been thrown or not, since the bedrooms looked as though they had been struck by a tornado. Baby toys, bottles, and other items were strewn over the beds and the floors. I really couldn't do much there by way of an investigation so, after looking around carefully, I returned to the living room. Chris was still standing where I had left her and, just as I reached the bottom of the stairs, another "pop" resounded.

"Oh my God," shrieked Chris. "It's starting again." She began crying and finally dashed out the front door in a panic to join her mother, as yet a third knock was heard. I bolted back up to the bedrooms immediately, only to be greeted by an icy silence.

It was clear to me now that the family was certainly being frightened by *something,* and there was every reason to believe that I would be able to witness the purported activity of the poltergeist myself if I stayed there long enough. I had also been intrigued by the popping sounds that were issuing from upstairs. I was pretty much convinced that I was witness to the antics of the poltergeist, and today, writing ten years later, I still feel that these initial sounds were paranormal in nature. The only problem was that I did not realize when I first entered the house that the structure was actually a duplex. So I cannot honestly dismiss the possibility that the sounds came from next door, traveled up the adjoining wall, and merely produced the illusion that they came from the second floor. But I consider this a remote possibility at best.

Since poltergeist infestations usually center on a young child around the age of puberty, this case was also fitting into a tried-and-true pattern. My attention naturally focused on Chris, who at thirteen was prime poltergeist material. So if I was up against a typical case of an "adolescent" poltergeist, I could be sure that the poltergeist phenomena would probably not occur unless Chris was in the house. I also realized that I had two main obligations while I was at the house. I certainly had the responsibility to investigate this possible poltergeist as thoroughly as possible and hopefully document it, but I also felt obligated to help the family cope with the ordeal they were going through.

These were just some of the thoughts that raced through

my mind as I stood looking into the upstairs bedrooms. The arrival of Raymond and Marjorie Bayless interrupted my introspection. Marjorie remained outside while Raymond came in to confer with me.

I immediately took him aside. "I think it's real," I whispered as Raymond nodded his head knowingly.

When Raymond and I are called to investigate a poltergeist, we are usually able to work out a research strategy in advance of our visit. But things were happening so fast in this case that it looked as though we would have to wing it. Being smack in the middle of an active case with very little preparation would obviously be a drawback, but I at least hoped that we could work up some sort of makeshift investigative procedure to use during our stay. So I pointed upstairs and we scurried up to talk about how we would handle the case.

The poltergeist was not about to give us a moment's rest, though. No sooner had we entered one of the upstairs bedrooms than we heard something bouncing down the stairs. We both rushed to the landing to find a lanolin moisture-cream bottle lying quietly at the bottom of the stairs, where it apparently had propelled itself. Mrs. Downs was at the foot of the stairs by this time, standing with her back to us. She was very hard of hearing and did not seem aware that anything unusual had happened. Her presence seemed suspicious, but it seemed unlikely that she would have thrown the bottle just to mystify us, since she was the one family member most frightened by the disturbances. But what about Chris, we thought, whom we could still hear talking in the kitchen? If she had run into the living room and thrown the object, we figured, certainly she would have been spotted by her grandmother. It seemed that this poltergeist wasn't about to be gun-shy.

Quiet reigned after this episode, which served as a temporary lull in the activity. This allowed us a little more time for the family to calm down, and it also permitted us to return upstairs to straighten up the messy rooms so that we could keep track of anything thrown about in the future. After we accomplished this somewhat domestic task, we returned downstairs to talk with the family members about just what they felt was going on, while

Marjorie left to go to the store to pick up some bread and cold cuts.

It was clear to us that all three women were frightened, haggard from lack of sleep, and hungry from lack of food. The activity had been so constant over the last few days that they hadn't even done their weekly grocery shopping. Unfortunately, it didn't take long to realize that there wasn't anything very enlightening that they could tell us. Since they had not kept a diary of the week-long events, we found ourselves incapable of evaluating the case on the basis of their combined testimony. We learned that the tappings on the front door (which initiated the disturbance) apparently ceased when the more dynamic outbreak commenced. There had apparently been dozens of incidents where household items catapulted about the house. This activity, accelerating over the last few days, had finally taken its toll on the family, who had found little time for sleep in the past forty-eight hours.

Since the poltergeist was at least temporarily in abeyance, Raymond and I went back upstairs to discuss exactly how we were going to handle the case. We decided that our best bet would be simply to hold vigil downstairs and see if the poltergeist would act up while we had the three family members under our direct surveillance. This procedure would at least rule out fraud. It is common for children in an infested house to sometimes "get into the act" by helping the poltergeist along a bit, so we realized that we had to be extra alert when Chris was moving about the house.

We went back downstairs with all these considerations in mind. It was now 6:30 P.M., and the poltergeist was about to play a little game of cat and mouse with us. We heard another one of those curious "popping" sounds from upstairs, and rushed up to see if we could find anything unaccounted for loose on the floor. We had hardly gone up the stairs and into the left bedroom when an incredible crash resounded right next to us on the landing. It almost sounded like a little explosion. I ran to the landing with Raymond close behind, and watched as a bottle bounced down the stairs. It came to rest at the foot of the stairs. It had apparently struck against the metal floor heater at the top of the stairwell, causing the explosive sound we heard.

This was actually one of the most impressive incidents that transpired during our stay. It was therefore doubly unfortunate that we didn't have the family under our direct surveillance at the time. Nevertheless, that someone in the family had engineered the incident struck us as unlikely. We had left them all in the kitchen and could still hear them talking there.

Since fakery was still a remote possibility, Raymond and I next decided to set a trap for the possible culprit. Since the family was still in the kitchen, Raymond and I staged a conversation, telling each other in loud voices that we would both go back upstairs and hold vigil in one of the bedrooms. We knew our conversation would be overheard. Then Raymond tromped noisily upstairs while I remained *on* the stairs to see if anyone would rush in to throw another object. No one followed the cue, and we could hear Chris, her mother, and her grandmother still talking in the kitchen. They were apparently impervious to our little trap. It was becoming clear that this case would not be easy to investigate, so I turned my back to go upstairs and notify Raymond that he might as well come back down.

That's when the cat-and-mouse game started up again. While I was still upstairs getting Raymond, we both heard a dull thud downstairs. We peered down the stairwell and there, lying by the living room coffee table, was a small lotion bottle. We had presumably heard it being tossed into the room from some other location in the house, and we could still hear the women talking among themselves in the kitchen. They seemed unaware of the incident, and we felt it better not to tell them. We reasoned that if the bottle had been thrown into the room by any one of them, the culprit would bring the episode to our attention and reveal herself. No one ever did, and the incident remained an enigma.

Marjorie returned to the house with some food as 7:00 P.M. rolled by. As we joined the family for some sustenance, we tried to convince them once again that the force they were confronting was frightening but, nonetheless, harmless. We advised them further that the events would probably soon burn out. Now, one strategy the investigator can use to help a family overcome a poltergeist attack is to help them understand the psychological nature of these infestations. If they realize that they are unconsciously unleashing the poltergeist force themselves, this knowledge alone will help extinguish the attack. We didn't feel that this strategy would work in this case, though. Tensions among the family members were so strong that we felt it was not the time to acquaint them with the psychodynamics of the poltergeist. Trying to convince them that they were producing the poundings and flying objects themselves would suggest to them that we were *blaming* them for the disturbance or charging them with fraud. We tried, instead, to persuade them that they should consider their house somewhat like an overcharged battery. Energy had built up in the house that was being released in a rather impersonal way, we advised, and they were unfortunately caught in the middle of the process. The family seemed puzzled by our make-shift explanation, but appeared relieved to hear us talk so calmly about the occurrences.

We were well into the evening hours by now. Since the family told us that the outbreaks did not usually carry over this late (except on the first day of the disturbance), Raymond decided to drive his wife home while I stayed on at the house. The women were still frightened and, since they really didn't want to be alone at night without someone around, Raymond and I agreed to remain for the night. Luckily, I was able to use Raymond's temporary absence to learn more about the family situation.

The story I heard was a sad one. It turned out that Mrs. James's second husband had deserted the family soon after the birth of her baby. Chris was her daughter by a former marriage, and it was clear that things had been very strained between the girl and her stepfather. She didn't seem to feel bad about his absence, and there were hints that he had been uncomfortable about his own attraction to this stunning teenager. I also learned for the first time that Mrs. Downs was not a regular member of the household, but was giving a helping hand since Mrs. James couldn't manage the baby and the home by herself. It was also clear that Chris resented her grandmother's presence, and felt that she was disrupting her bond with her mother already strained by the birth of the new baby. This was only one of the many stresses afflicting Chris, who was also unhappy about her

situation at school. Her classmates continually taunted her about
her mature sexual development, and the poltergeist was now
giving her a ready excuse to play hookey. Finances were also a
severe problem—the family was surviving on county assistance.

Poltergeist situations usually aren't very pretty. Certainly
the dynamics of this poor family's sad state of affairs made them
prime candidates for the stress and aggression that unleash such
poltergeist outbreaks.

My conversation with the family took about a half hour. But
then all my attempts to calm them down were abruptly stymied
by a dramatic incident. In a way, though, the cause of the ensuing
pandemonium was the first event that definitely proved the poltergeist was at least partly genuine.

It was now 9:06 P.M. I was sitting on the living room couch,
which faced toward the hall and stairway. Mrs. Downs was on the
couch next to me, while Mrs. James stood at the hallway entrance.
Chris was squatting by her side with her back leaning against the
wall next to the entrance. Both of them were directly in front of
me and motionless as I tried to cheer them up with stories about
some of my other psychic adventures. All of a sudden a tremendous bang exploded from the hall that sent all of us running. The
bang sounded as though a cherry bomb had gone off. Mrs. James
shrieked, "Oh God, the baby!" and ran about the living room in
a blind panic while I rushed into the hall. There I found a plastic
compact case lying by the wall opposite the downstairs bathroom.
(This bathroom was located between the kitchen and a back
bedroom.) It was clear that it had hurtled out of the bathroom,
smacked the wall, and produced the noise. The compact was
open but undamaged, and the powder puff was two feet away on
the floor by the bathroom door.

The entire incident posed an enigma. I could definitely say
that none of the women could have thrown the case, since they
were all in the living room with me at the time. Furthermore, the
noise made by the case on impact was horrendous. I could barely
imitate it by slamming my fist against the wall as hard as I could.
I had no idea how the object could have produced so much noise.
The position of the compact also presented a mystery. The plastic object struck with such obvious force that it should have been

smashed to pieces, yet it wasn't even chipped. Had the object been thrown against the wall normally, it should have bounced back away from it. But I found it resting right up against the wall even though the puff had been flung two feet away.

So what impressed me most was not only the circumstances under which this event took place, but also how it fell right into a typical pattern of the poltergeist. It is not unusual to find objects hurling into walls but not breaking, glasses falling but not shattering, tiny items falling but producing thunderous noises, as well as other enigmas. These are all added mysteries that highlight the bizarre disturbances, and my observations that evening were quickly convincing me that I was witnessing a genuine poltergeist display.

Mrs. Downs, Mrs. James, and Chris were running around the house in a frenzy while I was making my observations. This was understandable since the noise was more than a little startling. But it also put a crimp in my investigation, for if more poltergeist phenomena were to act up, I would no longer be in the position to verify their locations. So once again I had to ask the family to sit with me in the kitchen so that I could assure them that there was really nothing to be frightened about. I explained that I had personally studied such disturbances for many years, and that I had never known anyone to be physically attacked. I also pointed out that no serious injuries ever take place during the course of these outbreaks. (This was really a white lie, since some rather frightening injuries will occur on occasion. They only take place during very complex and vicious cases, and I had no reason to assume that this family was up against anything more than a rather mild and conventional outbreak.) People may get thumped, I acknowledged, but usually the offending objects just bounce off them harmlessly . . . even if they strike at high speed.

We discussed this issue as Chris, Mrs. Downs, and Mrs. James all huddled together around the kitchen table in a show of mutual support. To lighten the discussion a bit and to make a pertinent point, I told them a brief but amusing story about a colleague of mine who was once "attacked" by a poltergeist. The incident was reported by W. G. Roll, who has studied several poltergeist cases as project director for the Psychical Research Foundation in North Carolina. Bill was investigating a case in Newark where another family continually worried whether they would be injured by the flying knickknacks. He was advising them that they shouldn't worry and that poltergeists rarely attack people when—those fateful words just barely out of his mouth—a bottle came flying through the air and rapped him soundly on the head.* The family got a good chuckle out of the story, and I used this opportunity to make some notes on the compact incident.

My little talk must have amused the poltergeist as well as the family, for something struck my left pocket just as I entered the living room to get my notebook. Looking down immediately and somewhat startled, I watched as a plastic bottle-top bounced off my thigh. It fell to the floor a foot away. I could still hear the three women talking in the other room; they were obviously unaware of what had happened, and I only told them about it when they joined me in the living room later on.

But the poltergeist hadn't finished with us yet. A few minutes later Chris went into the kitchen and we heard a loud crash almost immediately. Mrs. James and I ran to the adjoining room where we found a bottle lying in a container of water that was placed on the floor. I was somewhat surprised when Mrs. James, almost in tears, began frantically accusing her daughter of causing the incident. Chris denied the charge and I was left totally puzzled. Why was the older woman, so sure only a few hours ago that a demon was loose in the house, now openly accusing her daughter of fraud? It just didn't make sense, but it alerted me once again to be on the lookout for fraud.

Raymond returned at about this time, and we suggested that the family get some sleep. They were harried, frightened, and exhausted. But at least they seemed comforted by our presence, and one by one they retired, leaving us to hold vigil.

What had we learned during our first day on the scene? It was certainly clear that our poltergeist was being elusive, for it usually

---

*This story is told by Roll himself in his *The Poltergeist* (New York: New American Library, 1973).

acted up only when our backs were turned. But this was not an insurmountable problem. In this respect it was lucky that I had been in the right place at the right time to witness one extremely evidential event; this was the incident with the compact. So I was sure that at least some of the activity in the house was genuinely paranormal. Some of the other instances we witnessed were impressive as well: the two bottles thrown down the hallway stairs; the cap incident; and some of the noises I heard when I first entered the house. The reactions of the women to these ongoing events were also just what I would have expected from a poltergeist-ridden family. They were terrified, and their anxiety was increasing with each additional outbreak of the poltergeist. Mrs. James's heart-rending concern for her 4½-month-old baby and Mrs. Downs's anguished calls to the local TV station were little "touches" almost as evidential as the object-throwings themselves.

Despite these positive aspects of the case, however, no one confronts the paranormal without at least some lingering doubts, since it is annoyingly common for the children in these troubled families to "help" the PK a bit after adjusting themselves to the shock of experiencing the unknown. It isn't odd to find the child throwing an object or two as the case progresses, so I still considered the "diagnosis" that we were on to a genuine case tentative.

There are several reasons for this maddeningly consistent pattern. Remember that a poltergeist is an outgrowth of family tensions and aggression, generally centering around one of the children in the home. These focal agents are usually frustrated, hostile, and aggressive, though they are prone to deny and repress these powerful emotions. This hostility and anger is invariably barred from entering conscious awareness and becomes locked within the confines of the unconscious. The poltergeist breaks forth when the child can no longer cope with these pent-up emotions, carrying out the very acts that the child would like to do normally. This is why poltergeists delight in pounding on doors and breaking things. The subconscious takes over so completely that the agent is usually not aware that he or she is actually the cause of the disturbance.

Now what does this have to do with fakery? To relieve

frustration, the agent will sometimes start manufacturing the poltergeist in order to more directly express his or her locked-up emotions. This psychological factor combines with the child's normal mischief-making tendencies in an unholy alliance. The child might also be receiving just the attention he or she has been denied in the past, so the child sometimes develops a vested interest in keeping the outbreak going.

There is even strong evidence that children who project poltergeist disturbances can fake the PK while in an abnormal state of mind, and may not even remember committing the transgression later.

All of these factors were very applicable to Chris, who was one of the most troubled teenagers I have ever seen. Inner hostility was pressuring her at every turn, but she could find no outlet by which to express it. She also seemed to be repressing a great deal of conflict over her burgeoning sexuality. She was a volcano of repressed anger—toward her stepfather (for his attraction and desertion/rejection); her mother (now caring for a new baby); and her grandmother (for disrupting the household with her presence). It was not hard to fathom why a poltergeist was erupting in this troubled home.

These thoughts were still in my mind when Raymond and I got up the next day. Several questions were unanswered as well, since we wondered whether the poltergeist had burned itself out the day before; or whether the family would be able to cope with any further disturbances. We also considered whether we should try prompting them into expressing their hostilities in order to (hopefully) kill off the poltergeist.

We also had another problem on our hands that was of even more direct concern to us. We were brought into the case by KTLA, who only reluctantly turned it over to us when they realized that they had no expertise in such matters. It was clear, though, that they expected us to cooperate with them in eventually filming a story on the outbreak. The idea of having cameras and newspeople invading the house during our investigation didn't exactly thrill us because it could well impede everything we were trying to do. But if the family gave the station permission to film, we could do nothing to keep them out. We wondered if they would call and if the family would cooperate with them, even if we counseled them that this was against our better judgment.

One by one the family arose from their first good night's sleep in two weeks and everyone was up by 11:15 A.M. When Chris came downstairs at 11:22, we knew we had to be on guard, for the poltergeist would awaken with her. It made its presence known about an hour later just as we anticipated.

The first incident of the day came while Raymond and I were in the living room. Suddenly there was a loud bang from the kitchen, where Mrs. James and Chris were fixing breakfast. We heard screaming and yelling as we ran to join them. We couldn't really determine what caused the noise, and Mrs. James was too frightened to answer our questions. It seemed that our poltergeist was being annoyingly elusive again.

Nothing else happened of any consequence until about an hour later. This time we were ready for it and were in a perfect position to authenticate the incident. Since this episode was so evidential, I'll have to describe it in some depth.

I was sitting on the living room couch and Chris was sitting on a chair to my right. The two older women were in the kitchen with Raymond, who stood at the kitchen door with his back to the hallway. No one was talking at the moment when—cling!—a metallic sound resounded. My eyes were immediately drawn to the hallway, where I saw a spoon bounce off the hallway door and fall into the living room. The door had been left open and flush against the wall, and Chris hadn't made a move. I was impressed by this incident, for even if she *had* somehow thrown the spoon while I was distracted, it wouldn't have bounced into the living room but into the hall. I also noted that, just as my eyes were drawn to the hallway, so were Chris's, whose mouth dropped open a bit in obvious amazement. It struck me at the time that her response was too spontaneous to have been staged.

The spoon incident was the prelude to what was to be about two hours of object-throwings. Some of the subsequent events came so fast and furious that it soon became almost impossible to chronicle, note, and document them. Chris went into the back bedroom as I was writing some notes on the spoon incident, and soon we heard a loud crash emanating from there. Chris could only tell us that a plastic container had flown across the room, and she then quickly joined her grandmother in the kitchen, while Mrs. James took sanctuary in the back bedroom with her infant. Raymond stayed with her so she wouldn't feel isolated.

I took up an observation post in the living room, and it wasn't long before I saw a glass fly from the kitchen and crash into the hallway wall, breaking and spilling milk everywhere. Chris and her grandmother were alone in the kitchen at the time, so the incident wasn't very evidential. They could only tell me that the glass had catapulted from the kitchen table when their backs were turned. I was forced to take their testimony at face value, but did notice something rather odd about the glass's flight. Some of the milk and a piece of tissue paper (which had been placed over the glass) were splattered over the refrigerator. The refrigerator was located between the kitchen table and the doorway, so the glass obviously ricocheted from the refrigerator into the hall. But it hadn't broken until it slammed against the wall. This didn't make sense since the object probably struck the appliance with greater force than it did when it bashed into the hallway wall.

By this time both Mrs. Downs and Mrs. James were beginning to get frightened again. They were in the same delicate emotional state in which we had found them the day before. Once again we heard talk of evil spirits, exorcism, and demon possession, so it was time that Raymond and I sat the women down and tried to explain what most parapsychologists believe a poltergeist to be. We spent a considerable time explaining that poltergeists are the direct results of pent-up emotions and frustrations. We did not earmark Chris as the source of the disturbances, since such a revelation would probably have frightened the girl. Nor did we want the other women to think that we were blaming the teenager for their problem. We also told them that the poltergeist, now that it was unmasked, would probably burn itself out quickly.

We thought we were doing a pretty good job of counseling the family when Mrs. Downs turned the table on us. She announced that she had called KTLA earlier in the day and that a news team was already on its way! Our hearts sank. The reporters' imminent arrival couldn't have been more badly timed, since the case, and our investigation of it, was at a critical phase now that we were forcing the family to take responsibility for the outbreak. They were beginning to work through their problems, or at least confront them, and any disruption to the psychodynamics we were orchestrating could be disastrous. There was only one thing I could do. I immediately went into the kitchen and got on the phone to the station's assignment editor and asked, demanded, and eventually pleaded with him to recall his reporters. But he insisted that the station had a right to the story.

This added tension probably delighted the poltergeist, and soon the disturbances started up once again. I heard a now-familiar crash as I walked out of the kitchen. A shattered mirror was lying at the end of the hall, but I didn't have time to investigate the episode, for already the news team was pulling up in front of the house. Since I knew I couldn't let them in without warning them about the delicate situation they were facing, I aborted my vigil to go outside and talk with them. A perfume bottle suddenly catapulted down the hall as I left the house, but no one bothered to note the family's position at the time, and I had more pressing matters to attend to.

The three-member news crew was just walking up to the house as I greeted them. Fortunately, I was able to intercept them and give them some quick counseling before they entered. My basic concern was to let them know that they were entering into a very delicate psychological situation and that they needed to make their visit as brief as possible.

The stage was now set for the grand entry of the news team, and lord only knows what they must have been thinking. Were they about to film a sequel to *The Exorcist*? Or a documentary on a lunatic asylum? My own trepidation about the filming took a turn for the worse when one of the team asked if he could film me doing an exorcism!

The smirks of the cameramen turned to looks of bewildered chagrin when yet another crash sounded from the rear of the house. Chris, her mother, and her grandmother soon came bolting up the hallway, so I interrupted my talk with the reporters to see what the commotion was all about.

It was then that I witnessed one of the more curious incidents of the day. I was alone in the back bedroom when I suddenly heard *another* small object flung against the wall behind me. The sound was unmistakable, though I could not discover exactly *what* had been hurled. There was just too much clutter and breakage all over the place. It was a very impressive incident, nonetheless, since it was the first to occur in a room empty of all family members.

No sooner had I written down a notation about this incident than a similar pop sounded from the hall.

Trying to keep accurate records of the case became impossible at this point. The object-throwings were obviously accelerating, the family members were running about every which way, and now we had three extra people (the TV reporters) in the house to contend with.

Finally, I felt forced to go back to the living room and ask the news people to get through with their work and leave. That's when Chris suddenly became very frightened and started running about the house, while several small objects propelled themselves through the air as though *following* her from room to room. This display lasted for about five minutes, after which Raymond was able to calm her. I would estimate that about four or five objects were thrown during the theatrics, and both Raymond and I were suspicious that the teenager may have thrown some of them herself.

This episode of poltergeist activity ended the current outbreak. The resulting quiet allowed the TV crew to finish their work, and they ended by asking Raymond and me for interviews. We knew the story would be aired regardless; so although we were reluctant to appear on film, we decided we would do more good than harm by explaining to the public just what a poltergeist represents. We tried to explain before the cameras that a poltergeist is not a demon or a spirit, but results from unconsciously projected psychokinetic energy meant to release psychological frustration. Our decision to cooperate at least helped smooth things over between the station and ourselves and, after we finished filming, Raymond decided to use the hiatus to drive home and freshen up. I decided to stay with the family.

It was now 4:12 P.M., and we had hardly recovered from all the excitement. Some residual poltergeistery was still active, so I suggested to Mrs. James (who was still very upset) that perhaps she should go back into the rear bedroom with her infant and close the door. I assured her again that no harm would come to her if she remained there alone. Meanwhile, Chris stayed in the kitchen with me while her grandmother went out for a walk. I sat down at the table, and positioned myself in such a way that the entire kitchen as well as the doorway were in my clear view. Conditions were now perfect for me to observe any further displays, and it wasn't long before I was rewarded.

I was just about to make a phone call (the phone was on the kitchen table) when Chris and I heard a loud wooden knock. The sound seemed to come from the hallway, and a brief investigation revealed that a bottle of fingernail polish had been thrown against the back bedroom door. This incident was certainly evidential, since the bedroom was on the same side of the hall as the kitchen. Even if Chris had somehow managed to throw the bottle, I wondered how she could have tossed it to curve in its flight and land by the door. Since I was facing the door from my position at the table, any idea that Chris evaded my observation in order to throw the object is rather far-fetched.

Chris joined her mother in the back bedroom and attempted to calm her down, while I wrote down some notes about the incident. These moments presaged what was to become the straw that broke the camel's back.

I was still writing when I heard glass shattering. A vase had suddenly smashed into one of the back bedroom's walls! It had been thrown with considerable force. Arriving barely an instant later on the scene, I found glass embedded a quarter-inch deep in the wall adjacent to where the vase had originally rested. Chris and her mother seemed terrified even though they had not actually seen the incident, and it took considerable time to calm them down. But this episode was one too many as far as the family was concerned. Mrs. James and her mother, who had just returned from her walk, decided that they couldn't remain in the house a moment longer. They wanted to leave even though they really didn't know where to go. I tried to reassure them, but neither of the older women were interested in my counsel any longer, and frankly I couldn't blame them. Being a parapsychologist, the poltergeist's antics naturally fascinated and challenged me, but I was forgetting how downright frightening such events can be to those untrained in their study. Because of the growing tension, I let down my guard as I spoke with Mrs. James and her mother. They were trying to get out the front door, which was jammed shut, so I had to turn my back on Chris in order to help them. Chris was sitting calmly in a chair next to a small table and lamp. They suddenly overturned with a resounding crash. I pivoted just in time to see Chris jump up as the furniture next to her fell to the floor. I must admit that I was immediately suspicious, since it appeared as though she had kicked the table over herself. I decided to keep my suspicions to myself, however, at least for the present.

With the other family members out of the house, I was alone with the teenager. I hoped that this would allow me to document more of the poltergeist. But KTLA called just then to get permission to use the film they had shot earlier in the day, so I had to go to the phone in the kitchen while Chris remained alone in the living room.

I was still talking on the phone when I heard a loud crash from the living room. I put the receiver down and ran into the other room, where Chris showed me that the stereo console had overturned. My suspicions were rekindled, since the poltergeist had never displaced such large objects before. They increased when Chris emphatically started denying that she could have pushed it over, even though I had not accused her of any wrong doing! To paraphrase Shakespeare, it struck me that "the lady protests too much." So I went back to the kitchen, phoned Raymond, and left a message with Marjorie for him to get back over to the house as quickly as possible. It was clear that I needed help, and some of my lingering doubts about the case were returning. I now wanted desperately to document at least a few more incidents, and I needed Raymond's help to do so.

By 5:45 that evening, Mrs. James, her mother, and the Baylesses were all back at the house. Everything was quiet. There were no paranormal antics for over an hour. And slowly Raymond, Marjorie, and I began helping the family fully adjust to their situation. We all sat together in the living room, and as we talked with the family, we learned about their needs and goals, as well as of their joys and frustrations. Finally, all the women went into the kitchen. When nothing further occurred over the next two hours, we were relieved to think that perhaps the psychic storm was over. But if the poltergeist's previous hurricane had blown itself out, a new storm was brewing.

Our surveillance of the family was slackening now, and at 8:45 we heard a sudden whisking sound from the kitchen and some startled exclamations. We ran to the kitchen where the family excitedly told us that a cap had flung itself along the floor. Two minutes later a similar event took place while Marjorie was still with the women. This time a mascara container was the target object and it, too, had suddenly whisked across the kitchen floor.

Since Raymond and I were in the living room at the time, we didn't witness this latest incident. But while jotting down some notes on it, Marjorie motioned to me with her eyes. "I want to talk to you upstairs," she whispered to me at an opportune moment.

Catching the sense of urgency in her voice, I stopped what I was doing in order to confer with her in one of the upstairs rooms.

There I was struck with the first clear accusation of fraud. Marjorie explained that, before the two incidents in the kitchen, she had told Chris that it was high time she went back to school, face her responsibilities, and stop hiding behind the poltergeist. Chris seemed annoyed at this prospect, immediately excused herself, and went into the bathroom. Marjorie was sure that Chris had palmed the mascara container and the cap while she was there and subsequently threw or kicked them under the table. Her feeling was that the teenager was doing this in order to stay home from school.

Marjorie's analysis of the situation seemed cogent. With the poltergeist apparently ebbing, it wasn't too outrageous to believe that Chris might now be exploiting the situation.

With these considerations in mind, Marjorie and I returned to the kitchen where Chris's behavior now betrayed her. She announced that she was going upstairs and wanted me to follow her. This seemed like an obvious ploy to keep me in good stead, so Marjorie interrupted her:

"No, you go along upstairs," she said. "Everything will be fine. There's no need for Scott to follow."

When she heard these words, Chris shot Marjorie the ugliest look I've ever seen pass from one human being to another. It was plain to me that the game was over and that Chris knew it. The likelihood that fraud was contaminating the case also placed Raymond and me in a considerable quandary. We admitted that some of the PK to which we had been witness could not have been faked, but we also realized that everything that was now occurring in the house had to be reevaluated. Only those incidents occurring in our direct presence, and when the family was under total control, could be considered genuinely paranormal. If our notes betrayed that Chris was unaccounted for during any given PK event, we would have to discount it as evidence for the paranormal. We also realized that Chris's probable fakery was a telltale sign that the poltergeist was withdrawing back into the deep recesses of her mind.

Chris seemed to sense our suspicions. We even caught her eavesdropping on our conversation as we discussed these matters in the kitchen. But the ultimate blowup was soon to come, and it was most revealing. Later that evening, Marjorie engaged both Chris and her grandmother in a dialogue that ended with Chris unleashing all of her hostility. She started yelling at us about all her hatred of her home, her family, and her life. All of her repressed hostility, anger, and frustration was released in a torrent of accusations and perjoratives. It was obvious to us that the poltergeist was over, since Chris's anger was finally finding a normal outlet. Chris was conquering it herself, perhaps with a little help from us. Our only job now was to help the family build up their psychological resources and overcome the ordeal that they had lived through. Raymond and Marjorie finally bedded down in the living room, and I left at 11:00 P.M. for my own home and some sleep. I had been in the poltergeist-infested house for thirty-one hours straight and it was time for a reprieve.

When I finally arrived home, I put my notes in order and

then fell into a sound sleep for a few hours. I was up again at the crack of dawn and back on the road to Mrs. James's house. The day was overcast, drizzly, and the atmosphere very oppressive. Frankly, the day couldn't have reflected my mental state better.

When I arrived back at the house, I found Raymond outside helping a passerby fix a flat tire. He greeted me solemnly and told me that after I had left Mrs. Downs admitted to him privately that her granddaughter was probably producing at least some of the object-throwings. She, too, was becoming aware of the teenager's complicity in the affair, although it looked as if Chris's poor mother still remained unsuspecting. Mrs. James was still in a daze after two weeks of continued horror, and we felt it totally inadvisable to tell her of our suspicions. We were afraid of her reaction were she to learn that her own daughter was "enhancing" the poltergeist's activity. Raymond's plan was to level with the girl privately; so when she came out of the house to talk with him, I excused myself and went inside. It was clear that some sort of confrontation was brewing, and it was up to Raymond to choose the best course of action.

Raymond told me later what was said during their impromptu meeting. He told Chris that the poltergeist was, in his opinion, over for good. He added sternly and knowingly, "I know it and *you* know it." The teenager looked at him inquisitively and asked him how he could tell. Raymond's response was to tell her that he could spell it out for her either politely or frankly, whichever she chose. The teenager apparently understood and didn't press the matter. Although no accusation of fraud was directed at her, she fully realized that we were on to her shenanigans. Raymond tried to soften their conversation a bit by reassuring her that she was an attractive and remarkable young woman, that she needn't have any worries about her appearance. He also assured her that we all liked her very much. Then he came to grips with the real crux of the matter, reminding her that her mother was in a bad emotional and financial state and that any more "antics" might break her mentally. He strictly enjoined her that ". . . no more incidents can *afford* to take place." He felt sure that Chris got the message.

Chris seemed much more friendly when she reentered the

house after her meeting with Raymond. She asked me whether *I* thought the poltergeist was over and if it would return? I told her that I agreed fully with Raymond, and added that poltergeists rarely come back after they abate. Chris seemed more joyful now and began sharing her records and rock-n'-roll magazines with me before retreating upstairs.

I stayed with the family all that afternoon. The poltergeist was usually the most active at midday, but the noon hours came and went in blissful silence. So at 3:30 P.M. I gathered up my notes and drove home. Raymond stayed on for a while to help the family adjust and to get Chris back into school. The poltergeist was apparently over, and so was our investigation.

To what extent was this poltergeist genuine and to what extent was Chris involved in perpetrating it by normal means? These are questions that, in retrospect, I have long tried to answer. During the course of my stay at the house, I was sure that I was witnessing several examples of genuine poltergeist activity. I still hold by this view. But to what extent Chris was consciously responsible for some of the incidents is a question I can't answer. It is my personal feeling that the serious fraud probably began while the television crew was on hand. That was about the time that the poltergeist began following Chris about the house in a rather suspicious manner. But I also believe that much of what Raymond and I saw during the first day of our investigation was authentic. The spoon and compact incidents could not have been faked, of that I am quite certain. But even today I turn the events of the case over and over in my mind, trying to sort fact from fraud.

The subsequent history of this particular poltergeist is not a very happy one. I eventually returned to the house twice in response to phone calls from Mrs. Downs, but was unimpressed by the incidents the family told me about. During one of these visits I even saw Chris try to throw a large ball down the stairway, only to stop dead in her tracks when she saw that I was watching her. The second time I returned to the house was on October 31, when Mrs. Downs called to say that all hell was breaking loose. The house looked like a disaster zone when I got there. Even the stairway bannister was ripped from the wall, but it was my opinion that Chris was once again acting out her hostility, as a clinical psychologist would term it. But I did witness one event that night that was very impressive. I had been greeted at the kitchen door by Mrs. Downs, who then accompanied me into the living room. While we were talking there, I distinctly heard a small object thrown in the kitchen. It was clear that Mrs. Downs had heard nothing owing to her poor hearing. Only a few seconds passed before Chris and her mother opened the door to the back bedroom and came out, so they could not have been the culprits. Soon Mrs. Downs went back into the kitchen and then called for me to join her. She immediately pointed to a bottle of fingernail polish lying in the sink, since she was puzzled as to how it got there. I consider this, even today, as one of the most impressive incidents of the case.

But it was the only remarkable incident I saw during my two subsequent trips to the house. Things grew rather strained between Mrs. Downs and me after this time, since she was developing the obsessive idea that I was writing a book on the case. Even though I emphatically denied any such plans, Mrs. Downs was insistent and started demanding money from me. Since she and the rest of the family were living on welfare, I could understand her need for financial assistance. It was also clear that she really believed I was trying to profit from the case. But her incessant demands for payment finally necessitated my withdrawal from further contact. I learned later that they were bilked out of $200.00 by a self-proclaimed exorcist who promised to rid them of their poltergeist once and for all. Several months later Chris ran away from home and was found living with a transient worker, who had been taken in by her good looks and maturity and had taken her for a girl of legal age. I heard nothing more about the case until more months later, when county workers were exploring the possibility of placing Chris in a foster home . . . much to her mother's emotional agony. It was a tragic end to a tragic story.

3

A Fiery Poltergeist in Simi Valley

Poltergeists certainly represent one of the most bizarre and baffling forms of psychic phenomena known to science. Brief, violent, and terrifying—they often rely on an incredible variety of tricks as they persecute the families in whose homes they erupt. Some poltergeists, like the one that attacked Mrs. James's family, like to throw household furniture around, while others prefer nothing better than to pound on walls and make other horrendous noises. A few poltergeists have been known to dematerialize household objects—such as knickknacks or bathroom vanity items—and teleport them away, only to rematerialize them later in totally senseless places. I know of one poltergeist that liked to steal the family's shoes and later deposit them inside their refrigerator freezer compartment. That really gave the family cold feet!

Not all poltergeists are that playful, though. They can become insidiously vicious. During a poltergeist siege in 1963, a family in Methuen, Massachusetts, was driven from their home when jets of water began springing out from the walls of the house. When they moved in with a relative, the same thing started happening there. But perhaps the most vicious of all is the *fire poltergeist.* These are poltergeists that start fires in the victims' homes and literally try to burn them out. Many such cases are on record in which sometimes dozens of fires have started, one after another. Thousands of dollars worth of damage has been caused by these poltergeists.

The fact that repeated spontaneous combustion is often the only phenomenon recorded in these cases has led some experts to question whether these outbreaks represent genuine poltergeists or not. I don't think there can be any question about it. Despite the unique and single-minded nature of the phenomenon, these fiery outbreaks follow most of the traditional patterns of the poltergeist. They usually erupt in a home that includes an adolescent, and will act up only when the focal agent is home. If the family tries to escape the fires by moving, the poltergeist will follow. Victims of the fire poltergeist often find their homes and temporary residences gutted no matter where they move. During some cases, the fires will combine with other, more traditional poltergeist effects.

So if you ever hear about a poor family that just couldn't keep fires from breaking out in their house, keep the poltergeist well in mind.

In some ten years of poltergeist hunting, I have only had the opportunity to study one such case: a fire poltergeist that broke out in a middle-class home in Simi Valley, a newly developing community on the outskirts of Los Angeles. Simi Valley is almost decadently middle class—the last place in the world you'd expect a poltergeist to visit.

The first information about the case came to my attention on March 9, 1976 (a day after the events began), when a story about it was run on the early (6:00 P.M.) edition of the local KNBC news. It merely announced that a Mr. John Eaton had reported a series of mysterious fires in his home. According to a release from the local fire company, fires had broken out one after the other in a phenomenally short period of time, and so far no cause had been found for the blazes. This was all the information the report offered, but it was all I needed. I smelled a fire poltergeist.

I was on the phone within minutes. My first call was to the local fire company. The station-house secretary was very cooperative and told me that, as far as she knew, Mr. Eaton had called the fire company very excitedly the night before. He had awakened from sleep to find a kitchen table on fire. A friend of his was visiting at the time, and the two of them had to put out several separate blazes that ignited in the house within a few minutes. She couldn't tell me anything more, since the inspector assigned to the case was still out on duty.

I was able to reach the fire inspector the first thing the next day, and he admitted to me that his investigation had as yet found no cause for the fires. But, he added ominously, he suspected arson on the part of the homeowner himself. In a way I was already beginning to sympathize with Mr. Eaton. The man had almost lost his home, and now the fire officials and police were about to charge him or his houseguest with arson. I explained my professional background to the fire inspector and also described the fire poltergeist syndrome, explaining that this possibility must be taken into consideration if charges were being contemplated against Eaton or his guest. I had no idea how the inspector would react to this suggestion. Fire departments, after all, get almost as many crank calls as police departments. The inspector, however, reacted just the way I hoped he would. He was intrigued. He asked me to send him a dossier on the fire poltergeist phenomenon and even gave me Eaton's address and phone number.

Two days later I was finally able to contact Mr. Eaton by phone. He didn't want any publicity but was eager to talk to anyone who might shed a little light on his ordeal. The next day, tape recorder in hand, I made the drive out to the suburb where Mr. Eaton lived, and learned directly from him what had happened.

Mr. Eaton turned out to be a very pleasant, unemployed white-collar worker. He was heavyset, clean-shaven, unmarried, and about thirty-five years old. He certainly didn't strike me as being a very likely candidate for a poltergeist attack. Poltergeists tend to erupt within family settings, often in those homes where adolescents are present. Mr. Eaton wasn't married—not to mention not having a family—and he was hardly an adolescent. My initial puzzlement was quickly resolved as my host explained just what had happened that fateful night. On the evening in question, a young friend of his had come to visit and they had talked and shared a few beers. Fred was twenty years old, and the two men were only casually acquainted. I naturally assumed that he was the likely agent. As the evening wore on Eaton retired to his room, while Fred "crashed" on the living room sofa.

That's when the poltergeist struck. Eaton woke up a few hours later and jumped out of bed when he smelled smoke.

"I was sleeping in the bedroom," he told me, "and I woke up and smelled smoke. I ran to the living room and I found the kitchen table—the bottom of the table—and chair next to it smoldering and burning. It was about 3:00 in the morning and I started pulling them [outside]."

Eaton went on to tell me that he immediately realized how difficult it would be to put the fire out, so he quickly opened a door that led from the kitchen into the backyard and dragged the still smoldering table and chair out of the house. He reentered the house, undoubtedly relieved that a fire had been averted. But he was in for a rude awakening. The poltergeist—or whatever the agent at work—was at it again.

"I came back in to open up all the doors to get the smoke out of the house," he continued, "and I saw that smoke was staying in the hallway. So I went back to my bedroom to open the windows there hoping to get the smoke out. That's when I saw that my bed was on fire. Fred was still sleeping on the couch and I had to rush back into the backyard to get my garden hose to put the fire out."

It took Eaton only a few moments to get the hose and pull it into the house. But the ordeal was just starting.

"When I came back in," he told me with a bit of cruel humor in his voice, "I saw that the corner of the couch was going up! Fred was still asleep and I woke him up by spraying him with the hose. The couch was actually flaming up."

With Fred awake, Eaton had at least a partner in his attempts to put the blazes out. Fred lunged from the couch and away from the fire, which might have reached his feet at any moment. Immediately sizing up the situation, he followed his host out of the living room and into the bedroom to help him spray the burning mattress. The mattress fire, though billowing with gobs of white smoke, was luckily not a serious one and was soon put out.

I was, of course, curious just where Fred was during this phase of the outbreak, but Mr. Eaton assured me that, from the time he first awoke him, Fred was never out of his sight.

A little more relaxed now, the two makeshift firefighters returned to the living room. But there they saw that a living room chair was now burning too, and threatening to ignite the entire living room! With the real prospect of a fiery inferno facing them, Eaton and Fred rushed back to retrieve the garden hose, lying in the bedroom, to put out this fourth fire, only to realize a moment later that an ottoman in the den adjoining the living room was now almost completely consumed in flames. They put this fire out, too, with little difficulty. This was the last fire of the evening and Eaton, finally with a moment to spare, called the fire department. The whole episode had lasted only ten to fifteen minutes, according to Eaton's calculation, and both he and Fred were totally perplexed by the fires and how they could have started. When the local fire officials arrived and heard the story, they were just as baffled by the rash of incidents, although Eaton expressed at least outward confidence that a normal cause would eventually be found for them. I was less sure as I spoke to both Eaton and the fire investigator on the case . . . and I don't think Eaton was too convinced of his own idea either.

"I don't really have any explanation for what happened," he told me toward the end of our meeting. "We're having a hard time explaining the fires. But I think someone got in and set them. I know the front door was locked. The only door I'm not sure about is the kitchen one. I don't know why anyone would do such a thing. The fire department looked around for quite awhile. I'm just getting an impression, nothing was actually said, but they think either Fred or I tried to start the fires."

Eaton's impression was right on target. The fire department investigator on the case, with whom I spoke several times, admitted to me during our first conversation that he suspected arson. He suspected Eaton in particular, and was contemplating turning the case over to the police. His theory was that Eaton had soaked the furniture with a combustible chemical, and later, while no one was looking, had set the fires with matches. However, the investigator refused to come to grips with the illogic of his argument. Why, I asked him, would Eaton have started the fires, only to put them out, and then call the fire department in fear that more blazes might break out? If arson were at the heart of the mystery, I didn't think Eaton was responsible. I still suspected a poltergeist at work, but there was always the possibility that Fred—this mysterious young man whom Eaton had only recently met—was the culprit, either normally or *paranormally*.

Fred remained a puzzling *persona dramatis* in this fiery drama. I was never able to interview him, and Eaton didn't know much about him. I called him several times but could never reach the young man. He and Eaton had met socially a week or so before, and this was the young man's first visit to the house. But Fred struck me as a suspicious character in one respect.

It seems rather unbelievable that Fred could have slept through at least two fires before having to be awakened by his host. One might suspect that he was setting the fires himself while Eaton's back was turned and feigning sleep when his friend turned to put out the blazes. That was my first reaction to the case. I became more sympathetic, though, when I learned that Fred was an extraordinarily heavy sleeper. I didn't have to take Eaton's word for it either. The fire inspector told me that the young man had fallen asleep as he was being interviewed and couldn't be awakened! But let's take a closer look at the fires themselves.

There were at least two blazes that I don't think Fred could have started. He was in the bedroom with Eaton when the living room chair began to burn, and he was in Eaton's direct presence when the ottoman ignited. Step by step, I went over the night's proceedings with Eaton, and ended up fully convinced that neither of the two men could have set the fires unobserved by the other. I also gleaned some clues about the nature of the fires when I examined the furniture that had been burned.

Whatever caused the fires, it must have generated intense heat. When I inspected the pieces of furniture that had been damaged, I found that many of them were charred or consumed over large surface areas. Yet Eaton claimed that he had been able to put the fires out quickly. Only the couch was superficially singed. What was most intriguing was that the mattress was very peculiarly burned. The box springs were much more damaged than the mattress itself, so it was very clear to me that the fire had first ignited the box springs, which had then *burned up into the mattress.* If the fire had been deliberately set, it would have been easier to set fire to the mattress itself. The table, too, had first begun burning from the bottom, and the chair seemed to have combusted from *within* its stuffing before spreading outward. Strange indeed.

The locations of the fires also pose a curiosity. Although the first fire broke out in the kitchen, the remaining four blazes followed in a patterned sequence. They broke out in (roughly) a straight line, moving right through the house, beginning in the bedroom and ending in the den. This pattern became very clear when I noted the fires on a floor plan of the house. (See diagram.) So the fires weren't random, but seemed to be ignited by some "force" moving directionally through the house. This is certainly the most meaningful clue I discovered about the fires, and it would be interesting to see if other fire poltergeists conform to a similar pattern. Unfortunately, we just don't have enough data on any other cases to make this determination.

I discussed these various details with Mr. Eaton during our meeting and finally explained the nature of the poltergeist to him, telling him about some fire poltergeists that were on record. He wasn't too thrilled with my theory, however. He didn't believe in the supernatural, he told me, and only wanted to know "who" had started the fires and why. That's something neither I nor the fire department could tell him.

Luckily, the arson theory was not pursued. I don't know how much I had to do with it, but the officials with whom I spoke began to grow more and more intrigued by what I was telling them about fire poltergeists. They admitted that it was a possibility, but also pointed out that they had never learned about such a phenomenon when they were in training. In conclusion, it still seems to me that Fred could have been the paranormal cause of the fires. Most poltergeists, fiery ones and otherwise, focus on an adolescent and Fred, at age twenty, was still within the range for

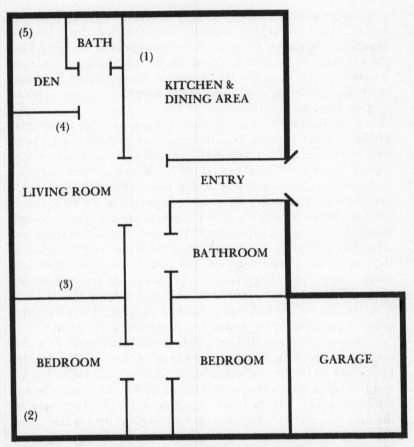

SCENE OF THE FIRES: (1) Table and chair; (2) Bedroom mattress; (3) Living room couch; (4) Living room chair; (5) Den ottoman.

a "poltergeist child." There is only one puzzling aspect to this theory. Many poltergeist experts point out that these psychic attacks usually do not erupt when the focus person is asleep. This point is made by Dr. A.R.G. Owen, former Cambridge University geneticist, in his book *Can We Explain the Poltergeist?* and is echoed by W. G. Roll in his own book *The Poltergeist.* This case appears to have been an exception.

Nonetheless, this incident does fit the typical fire poltergeist profile in many respects, even though it was so short-lived. There have been over a dozen reported and well-witnessed cases in the United States and Canada since 1930. They've occurred in Kentucky, Montana, Nova Scotia, and in many other locations. Dozens more have probably never been reported at all. In a typical case, anywhere from three to thirteen fires are produced, though sometimes there will be too many to count. Fire poltergeists are also extremely short-lived, and many cases last only a couple of days or weeks. More conventional poltergeists will often last much longer. Most frightening of all, many fire poltergeists do not end their assault until they've burned down the victim's home. Eaton, at least, escaped that fate, although his poltergeist seemed quite intent on destroying his house at the time.

The strange fires that struck Mr. Eaton's middle-class home are still an unresolved mystery. It has never been solved by Mr. Eaton nor by the fire department. Mr. Eaton still thinks that an arsonist snuck into his home that fateful night, but he can't figure out how or why. I can't, however, agree with him. The cause of the fires was probably far more mind-boggling than either he or the local fire inspectors truly cared to consider.

4
Gremlins in a Hollywood Factory

In his entertaining book *A Dictionary of Ghost Lore,* Peter Haining writes that "recently there have been stories of gremlins making their presence felt in large factories." He adds that "from this suggestion has emerged the theory that they may be entities somehow formed by the working of machines."

Gremlins . . . or poltergeists?

The assault tactics upon which the poltergeist so often relies are varied and awesome. Rock throwing, violent psychokinetic displays, fire, teleportation, and even biting (!) are all phenomena for which it has a peculiar penchant. A poltergeist may rely either on a battery of such tactics or on one exclusively. Nor is it rare for a poltergeist to commence its disruptions with one approach before widening its repertory of antics. Probably the least recognized or appreciated of all poltergeist types is, however, the "electronic" poltergeist. These cases often go undiagnosed, but they make their presence known by causing machinery and equipment either to malfunction inexplicably or to behave oddly. Just as with your more traditional poltergeists, they usually revolve around an individual and often attack their victim both at work and at home. Mucking up complicated equipment is a specialty of this bothersome visitor, and the attacks generally focus on high-power or electrical equipment. This is why they are called "electronic" poltergeists. Other researchers have suggested that they be labeled "proto-poltergeists," since they sometimes do not escalate into object-throwings or display other types of overt psychokinesis.

The following two brief case descriptions will give you an idea of what these electronic poltergeists can be like.

The most celebrated of all electronic poltergeists was no doubt the Rosenheim case of 1967, named after the Bavarian city where it occurred. The scene of the attack was a lawyer's office, which seemingly became overrun by gremlins. The office telephones began going haywire, fuses blew out for no reason, lights blinked on and off mysteriously, and phone calls that were never actually made started registering on the office phones—sometimes more rapidly than anyone could humanly dial. The lawyer in charge had little idea what was going on, so he called in representatives of the local power company. They checked over all the power inputs and even hooked up an emergency power supply to the building. Nothing seemed to help, and the electronic disturbances continued right along as before. Even the emergency power unit began to fluctuate wildly, as though some invisible energy were interfering with it. By this time the local authorities were totally baffled by the case, and in desperation they called upon Dr. Hans Bender from the Institute for the Study of Border Areas of Psychology in Freiburg. Dr. Bender, Germany's leading authority on the poltergeist, lost no time determining that the problems all revolved around the presence of a teenaged office worker. Only when this young lady was present did the mischief become so frantic.

With its nature fully exposed, the poltergeist no longer hid its true identity from view. Soon violent psychokinetic storms burst out in the office. Lights suspended overhead would swing ominously; a huge and heavy filing cabinet pushed itself away from a wall; and pictures hung on the walls would rotate by themselves. The activity only ceased when the woman around whom it was focusing left to seek other employment. The poltergeist continued to plague her, however, and her boyfriend later complained that the electronic pinsetters went haywire whenever they went bowling! The source of the trouble seemed to be the girl's poor adjustment to her work and to her personal (love) life.

The odd power surges that played such a conspicuous role in the Rosenheim case are not unique. Only two years before the case hit the press, a similar occurrence had been reported from my home state of California. The *Los Angeles Times* ran a short story on March 1, 1966, about a house in the Ojai Valley (located several miles north of Los Angeles) where electronic gremlins were at work. The homeowners had complained to the Edison Company because of a rash of light-bulb explosions in the house. Monitors placed on the power lines revealed that power surges were forming within the house and were the probable source of the disturbance. What puzzled the company was that no similar surges were recorded on the lines just outside the house.

This background information should help prepare you to appreciate the peculiar "electronic" poltergeist Raymond Bayless and I confronted in the summer of 1978. It was holding forth in a huge plastics factory in Hollywood, California. We first learned of the case in July when an employee of the company, Ms. Gladys Gordon, called Raymond Bayless at the suggestion of the Southern California Society for Psychical Research. She described all sorts of electronic hi-jinx attacking the building where she worked, adding that no one seemed capable of helping her. Sometimes her phone went haywire or the call buttons would light up in frantic sequences. Weird wailing noises would often come over the public address system during these episodes. She had also gradually discovered that these annoying, though luckily harmless, outbreaks only occurred when she was present in the building.

The case didn't sound all that promising at first. But Raymond sensed that there might be more to it, so we decided to keep close tabs on the situation.

Raymond and I had an opportunity to witness these outbreaks firsthand on July 21, when Ms. Gordon placed a frantic call to Raymond. Things were acting up again at the plant! Raymond called me up immediately and asked me to join him there. I was delighted since his call gave me a perfect opportunity to put aside the rather dull book I was reading that afternoon. Because of the plant's location, we decided to take separate cars.

Since my knowledge of the case was relatively small, it struck me at the time as merely a curious anomaly. But it seemed worth a look. Raymond was able to make better time than I was, so he arrived at the scene of the disturbances at 3:30 P.M. I drove up about forty-five minutes later. My colleague had already made contact with Ms. Gordon, and they were both waiting for me at the reception desk where they hastily filled me in on the day's activities. The electronic interference that day had been particularly intense, I learned. Especially bad were the awful and totally inexplicable noises emitted from the plant's paging system. Even the other employees were now aware that the problem was somehow linked to Ms. Gordon, which was obviously causing her a great deal of distress. Raymond broke in at one point in our talk and explained that Ms. Gordon had left the building for several minutes right before his own arrival. Her departure, according to many of the other employees, caused a prompt cessation of the noises.

Of course we didn't know it at the time, but we were just about to witness the disturbances for ourselves. But before describing the rest of our visit, I would like to backtrack and explain a bit about the strange history of this case. This information will help you to keep the rest of the account in proper perspective.

It turned out that the plant had always had a fair share of problems. Long ago it had been learned that the manufacturing equipment used there emitted an intense output of radio waves, requiring that the equipment be heavily shielded. The plant's operations had in the past even caused some problem with the functioning of a flight control tower at a nearby airport, where the communication system was obviously crucial to air safety. Despite the installation of formidable shielding, there was still an abnormally high rate of radio-wave emissions present in the factory. The emissions were so bad that they could render a tape recorder inoperable. Some of the factory workers and staff even claimed that they could "feel" the emissions.

These radiations were, of course, blamed when the first disturbances struck the plant earlier in 1977. The present rash of incidents—which dated from May of that same year—was not the first of its kind noted by the factory workers. Similar disturbances had been reported, but those attacks had plagued a different female employee and *not* Ms. Gordon. Although the the intercom system was never affected, this employee's telephone system continually went on the fritz until new equipment finally had to be installed in desperation. No one in the plant at first linked these prior problems with the current disturbances, and no one even thought them strange until the present difficulties arose. What was now so odd was that the disruptions were obviously focusing directly on Ms. Gordon. The plant's general manager later told us that he personally watched one day as Ms. Gordon's electric typewriter and calculator went berserk during one of the electronic attacks.

The electronic disturbances noted during the previous summer were so bad, in fact, that the plant manager had to call in a trouble-shooter from a local company specializing in communication systems. His first plan of action was to install new equipment in that part of the plant reporting the difficulties. But this strategy didn't work out too well, since the new equipment started acting just as oddly as had the older (and allegedly "malfunctioning") equipment. This situation struck the troubleshooter as so strange that he began studying the matter in some depth. He and his company continued their work by replacing Ms. Gordon's desk phone, because this system seemed to be the focal point of the disturbances. The station buttons at the base of the phone were especially checked out, isolated, and monitored. But the phones and the light still went crazy during the electronic attacks, and the trouble-shooter finally admitted defeat when he couldn't determine the cause.

"There are only certain basic things that happen in telephone equipment," he was to tell Raymond months later, "and once you have checked these functions, then you know that you have done everything to correct anything normally out of order."

In light of the growing mystery surrounding the gremlinlike antics, someone finally decided that perhaps parapsychology would succeed where electronic expertise had failed. This brainstorm was the direct reason for our July-21 visit. Ms. Gordon had located Raymond after consulting with another local parapsychologist and the Southern California Society for Psychical Research.

But now back to the present.

When I arrived and checked in at the plant's appointment desk, meeting Raymond there, Ms. Gordon explained a little about the current problem and then escorted us down a corridor and into her small office. It was constructed from dry-wall partitioning, and a couple of small plants decorated the otherwise antiseptic room with its metal desk, electric typewriter, phone, and file cabinets. The poltergeist—or whatever it was—actually flared up while Ms. Gordon was explaining how any phone she touched would inevitably become jinxed. She was telling us how she even seemed to sense when an outbreak was coming, explaining that she could ". . . feel it in my body." She linked these sensations to the radio emissions in the building. It was 4:47 in the afternoon by this time, and the show was ready to begin. It was quite a display!

It began when a paging speaker right outside the office in which we sat and near the ceiling began to emit an ear-splitting, high-pitched wail. We all dashed into the corridor when the sounds first assaulted us, and we could hear that the same sounds were coming out of all the speakers along the corridor. The entire system was affected.

"Now my phone will start up," said Ms. Gordon almost nonchalantly as we went back into her office. The speakers were still wailing away. And sure enough, suddenly her phone did begin to act very oddly. The several call buttons at the base of her phone started lighting up in rapid and random fashion. Several sequences came per second and served as a grotesque ballet to the intercom's ugly concert.

"I bet the same noises are coming over the phone," she then added.

While remaining just as calm as can be, Ms. Gordon picked up her desk phone and handed it to Raymond. He nodded and then handed it to me. The same wailing noises that were shrieking along the corridor were indeed coming through the phone. What was so truly bizarre was that the *public address system and the factory telephones were separate systems—there was no way, mechanically or electrically, that one system should normally affect the other.* What we were witnessing was mechanically impossible.

We hung up the phone and picked it up again several times over the next few minutes. The noises coming through the receiver never ceased. Then suddenly at 4:49, the commotion ended.

Momentarily, it seemed that peace and quiet had returned to the factory. But the quiet didn't last long. Within moments a second outbreak commenced. Once again it was the paging system that acted up first, followed by the now familiar telephonic antics. We tested the phone several times during this second outbreak, and found that the pattern of the disturbances was somehow changing. Sometimes wailing sounds would come over the receiver, while on other occasions we found the phone to be totally dead. This eruption only lasted for a few minutes, so we weren't able to experiment much with the gremlins responsible. Raymond, however, was able to make a few interesting observations on the basis of the episodes we witnessed. He noted that a small electric clock on Ms. Gordon's desk ran smoothly despite the problems with the phone and paging system, thus indicating that the disruptions were selective and did not pervade all the power inputs to the factory. He had also brought along a compass to see if it would detect any peculiar electromagnetic oddities during the sieges. It didn't.

Raymond and I were able to witness a third outbreak of the activities at 5:07, although this flareup was much less intense and was confined solely to the intercom system. Ms. Gordon, Raymond, and I left the building shortly after this display, which apparently ended the day's noisy activities. Probably the most novel observation we were able to make was that Ms. Gordon's desk clock worked normally despite the day's antics. This indicated that the poltergeist was intelligently *choosing* which aspects of the plant's channels to disrupt.

There was, unfortunately, rather little we could do to further investigate this case. We simply didn't have the equipment, resourses, or expertise to mount a major investigation. So we could do little more than keep abreast of the case and its subsequent developments. Raymond ended up doing a great deal of footwork by interviewing other witnesses at the plant, representatives of the company that had tried to correct the problem, and the plant management. He even paid a second visit to the factory on September 19 in answer to a call from his contacts there. This visit enabled him to witness a small-scale repeat of our July-21 adventures.

My own involvement with the case was reduced to finding a psychological cause for the disturbances. My plan was to determine if the disturbances were related or linked to some trauma or conflict buried in Ms. Gordon's mind. Such a finding would definitely link the episodes to the poltergeist, and would eliminate the idea that the disturbances had a normal (though as yet undiscovered) source.

This approach ultimately hit pay dirt. By interviewing Ms. Gordon in some depth, it gradually became apparent that she was uncomfortable with her job because of her personal relationship with her boss. She even admitted to me that the disturbances seemed to specifically collate with times of stress in her private life. The case was obviously running true to form . . . if not phenomena . . . for the poltergeist. But there simply wasn't much else we could do, and I had a difficult time pinning Ms. Gordon down for further tests.

The last we heard of the case came some weeks after our visit, when Ms. Gordon informed us that similar difficulties were now plaguing her home and even her car radio. The problems continued well into 1979. But by this time the plant directors decided that they didn't want any outsiders interfering with their "internal" affairs. Our access to information about the case was therefore cut off. We never learned anything more about the ultimate disposition of this most curious poltergeist.

The actual mechanics of this case were complex as well as intriguing, despite our limited involvement in the overall investigation. The outbreaks never evolved into pure poltergeist events, but the case adhered to the patterns typical of the poltergeist rather well.

Here we had a case in which inexplicable physical occurrences were erupting in a building, focusing on an unhappy employee working there. Nothing could be more "poltergeistic."

It was Raymond's final opinion that this case actually represented a form of proto-poltergeist. He came to this conclusion when he discovered that, as cited earlier, a previous employee had also been victimized by similar disturbances some months prior to the current difficulties. He linked this coincidence to the fact that radio-wave emissions were so strong in the factory. Raymond couldn't dismiss the strong possibility that there was a significant relationship between the facts that the disturbances could be traced to *two* human sources, and that both of these young women claimed they could actually "feel" the radio emissions within their bodies. These facts allowed him to construct a tentative theory about the case. As he states in his official report on the case:*

> It seems very unlikely that two unrelated individuals in the same area at different times and not in the presence of each other, can be "poltergeist agents." Therefore, I suggest that this may be a protopoltergeist case caused in part by familiar physical processes—in this case actual radio wave emissions, electromagnetic fields or transmissions. The two young women involved were, I suspect, acting as detectors who modulated radio waves into a form that could be picked up physically on electronic equipment, such as telephones and speakers. The "raw material" for the phenomena encountered here was actual radio wave emissions. I think that this case can be described as a protopoltergeist disturbance since its close relationship to normal physical phenomena perhaps removes it from the poltergeist category *per se.*

These views are certainly provocative. We later learned that a similar case—this one additionally including object-movements—had broken out in the Bronx, New York, in 1971, long before our own investigation. One of the investigators on that case was Dr. John Artley, an engineer from Duke University. He, too, came

---

*Raymond Bayless, "An Electronic 'Poltergeist'?" *Theta*, 8 (1980), 9–11.

to the conclusion that radio waves were somehow responsible for the disturbances. He was even able to register these minute emissions by placing a radio receiver near an object moved by the poltergeist minutes before. Later he was able to confirm this observation, the emitted radiations being at 146 MHz.

My own feelings about Ms. Gordon's proto-poltergeist are a little more exotic. I feel Raymond's speculations are probably only half-true or partial, as he himself admits. It seems likely that while the radio waves were the raw source of the problem, some sort of PK process must also have been at work. In other words, I think it likely that somehow Ms. Gordon psychokinetically transformed the raw energy given off by the emissions and then transformed and redirected them in order to cause the problem. The same may have been true of the earlier employee. The psychokinesis in both cases may have been working *via* the radio waves. This curious view is based on the fact that the disturbances were somehow being clearly manipulated by Ms. Gordon's subconscious mind—that is, during those times when she was undergoing particular psychological stress. Psychokinesis is, to a large degree, an unconsciously mediated force. If the cause of the problem were merely the radio waves themselves somehow *normally* modulated by Ms. Gordon's body (as Raymond seems to be implying), this psychological connection shouldn't exist. The outbreaks should have been more random; nor should they have occurred in her home or car in addition to the factory. Somehow the employee had to be doing *something* to cause the disturbances, and their intelligent action was undoubtedly PK-related. While the radio waves gave the poltergeist its energy source, Ms. Gordon's innate PK capabilities probably gave it its direction and means of expression.

Further evidence supporting this view comes from those many cases, such as the Rosenheim incidents, when electrical disturbances escalated into object-throwings and other manifestations. The factory in which Ms. Gordon worked was thankfully spared such an annoying ordeal.

5

Tucson's Rock-Throwing Phantom

"I can't even come home and enjoy a beer anymore," lamented forty-five-year-old Richard Berkbigler. He was looking at the cement floor of his half-finished home as he spoke, trying momentarily to ignore the twenty or so reporters, friends, and self-appointed vigilantes who were invading his house. They were all there to help his family hunt down the phantom "prankster" that had been throwing rocks at his home for ten weeks.

Rock-throwing poltergeists represent a specific type of spookery. These noisy and rackety ghosts don't engage in your typical poltergeist behavior. They don't rap on walls, throw household furniture about, or cause knickknacks to disappear and reappear. Instead they delight in pelting the houses they attack with rocks. They can make the stones shower from the sky in a nefarious rainfall, or they will simply pelt the building. The rocks will even fall inside the home on rare occasions. Sometimes these displays will be accompanied by more traditional poltergeist activity as the case escalates, but usually the phantom rock-throwings will represent the only strategy of attack. This was the type of case I confronted in December 1983 when I heard about a possible stone-throwing poltergeist holding forth in a desert home outside Tucson, Arizona. When I arrived on December 6, the poltergeist was still active, kicking up as big a fuss as ever.

This case did not turn out to be as dramatic as many others of this genre. Rock-throwing poltergeists have a habit of becoming quite bizarre. It is not odd for the rocks to fly abnormally slow, zigzag in flight, or even make ninety-degree turns in the air. This poltergeist turned out to be somewhat less eccentric, although this came as little comfort to the family living in the besieged house.

For Mr. and Mrs. Richard Berkbigler and their family, the nightmare had all begun three months earlier in September. They and three of their five children had been living in a trailer for over a year on five acres of desert property they owned. Despite the fact that their large 4400-square-foot house was only partially completed by then, the Berkbiglers had decided to move in anyway. They were relieved to get out of the cramped trailer even though their new home had only concrete floors instead of carpeting and no doors on any of the rooms. But the move into their dream house turned sour when the rocks started hitting. Only a few days after setting up housekeeping, Richard and Mary Berkbigler and their children—Rick (aged twenty), Anita (aged nineteen) and David (aged fifteen)—were annoyed when rocks started hitting the front of the house one evening. The stones were large, about fist size, and a number of them struck the house directly while others dented the family van parked on a large dirt clearing in front of the house. Richard and his sons ran out to find the culprit responsible, but they couldn't see anyone nearby. This didn't strike them as odd, because their house is bordered by hundreds of square yards of bush, cactus, and underbrush. Nor are there any other houses on their property.

The Berkbiglers tried to put the night's episode behind them, but the rock-throwings got worse over the next several weeks until it was a daily occurrence. The attacks usually began in the evening between 5:30 and 7:00, generally just before or after Mr. Berkbigler arrived home from his work as a truck driver. His children and his wife—who owns her own cleaning establishment in Tucson—were usually already home by that time. At first the rocks would plop down on top of the roof, but as the incidents escalated the rock-throwings became more vicious. The missiles would start striking the house in brief flurries; five or so rocks would strike the front of the house or their van at two- or three-second intervals. There would then be a brief hiatus of about five to fifteen minutes, and then another flurry would begin. Sometimes these rocky barrages would be somewhat sporadic and brief, but on other occasions the attacks would go on for two or three hours. The Berkbiglers usually scurried outside in hopes of catching sight of their prowler when the first stone hit, but they never could find anyone. They sometimes were even struck by the rocks as they searched. The attacks would only stop when the family turned off all the lights in the house and simply went to bed.

Neither Mr. Berkbigler nor his sons were too puzzled by the incidents at first. They believed that a vagrant had probably been living in the house before they moved in and was trying to scare them out. Even during the escalation of the rock-throwings, the family maintained this idea. When I first met them some two months or so later, they explained that they had good cause to believe that someone was determined to drive them from the house. Before actually moving into the house, a refrigerator had been installed in the partially completed kitchen. Food was kept there to supply the trailer in which the Berkbiglers were living, and often they found some of this food missing. They assumed (reasonably enough) that a vagrant sheltering in the house was stealing it, and wanted his unwilling hosts gone. Most of the Berkbiglers accepted this without question; but as the attacks went on day after day, Mrs. Berkbigler began entertaining different sentiments.

"Maybe it's a spirit," she told reporters from the *Arizona Daily Star* at one point. "Maybe we've built over some sacred burial grounds or something."

No one else in the family was very sympathetic to this idea, though, and her husband often seemed irritated by his wife's tentative "superstition."

Since the rocky barrages were continuing on a daily basis, even the local press started dubbing the culprit the "phantom" stone-thrower because of his uncanny ability to evade detection.

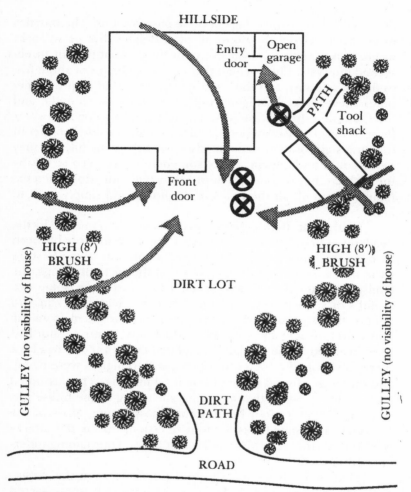

HILLSIDE

Entry door

Open garage

PATH

Tool shack

Front door

HIGH (8′) BRUSH

HIGH (8′) BRUSH

GULLEY (no visibility of house)

GULLEY (no visibility of house)

DIRT LOT

DIRT PATH

ROAD

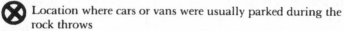 Location where cars or vans were usually parked during the rock throws

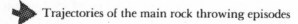 Trajectories of the main rock throwing episodes

The local sheriff's substation was contacted by the Berkbiglers in early November, and deputies were sent on several occasions to help ferret out the perpetrator. Helicopter surveillance was employed during some of these searches, but the prankster—whatever his nature—always managed to elude detection. In fact, the sheriffs eventually became rather reluctant to venture up to the Berkbiglers' property at night when they, too, started getting struck by the rocks. One deputy told the *Daily Star* that the rocks had done $600.00 damage to his patrol car.

The Berkbiglers were just about at their wits' end when I learned about the case. The story of their plight was being featured in the *Daily Star* where it came to the attention of Susy Smith, now retired after a long career of writing books on the paranormal. She immediately contacted W. G. Roll at the Psychical Research Foundation in Chapel Hill, North Carolina. He, in turn, contacted me in Los Angeles on December 6 and asked if I could look into the matter. I was on a plane for Tucson by 10:20 A.M. the same day, and arrived at the troubled house at 3:00 in the afternoon. It was a long drive from downtown Tucson out into the desert north of town and through a series of half-flooded roads. When I finally arrived, a small group of people were already there. A carpenter was working away merrily in the open attached garage, while two reporters from the *Tucson Citizen* were already waiting for the first rock of the day to fall. Two young professional animal trackers were also waiting, but the only member of the family at home was Rick, the Berkbiglers' oldest son. I explained who I was to the delight of the bored reporters and to the amusement of the trackers. Rick was hospitable and immediately took me inside and filled me in on the case as the other members of the family gradually arrived over the next few hours.

Rick explained to me that the prankster, poltergeist, vagrant, or whatever, had been particularly nasty all week. He and his parents were now welcoming anyone who could help them put a stop to their ten-week ordeal.

It wasn't enough that the house was being pelted daily by the rock thrower, Rick went on to explain, but during the last week it had begun picking off people with amazing accuracy. The chronology of events Rick told me was truly amazing.

The heavy attacks all began a week or so earlier—on Sunday, November 27. It was one of those days when the rocks just wouldn't cease. The Berkbiglers and several of their friends and relatives were home that night, and finally a group of the men decided to hunt down the culprit once and for all. Rocks were still striking the house and the cars from the pitch-black desert when Rick started organizing two search teams. Rick, who was trained in the Marine Corps Reserves, knew his strategy well. He recruited three of his friends and set out to search the brush and gully to the south of the house, while he instructed his uncle and three other volunteers to similarly stalk to the north of the house. Rick's idea was to trap the prankster between them when they met at the rear of the property. Since it was 8:30 at night and totally dark, both teams took along flashlights. They began their search when it appeared as though the rocks had gone into one of their frequent abeyances. But they didn't have long to wait before the rock-throwings commenced with renewed vigor.

Rick and his friends were scouring the south property adjoining the house when the phantom threw his next stone. A large rock came flying out of the desert and struck one of his team members squarely and painfully in the jaw. The attack unnerved the young men, who quickly walked behind the house to get out of the culprit's range. No sooner had they positioned themselves to the rear of the house than they heard Rick's uncle calling to them. He and his men were still at the north of the house and they had pinned the rock thrower down in a clump of bushes about twenty-five feet from the building. They could still hear rustling in the brush.

Both Rick and his uncle shined their flashlights into the brush, but there was simply nobody to be seen. Suddenly, however, a flurry of about eight rocks came flying right out *from* the brush.

"It was just like the bush was throwing rocks with its branches," the twenty-year-old, part-time college student told me.

One of the rocks struck Rick's uncle in the temple, knocking the man unconscious by the impact. Rick and his friends started pelting the bush (with its puzzlingly invisible prankster inside) with rocks as the other men helped the injured stalker back to the house. Neither Rick nor any of his friends saw the prankster leave the brush, and they, too, gave up their assault to see to the injured man. More rocks struck the house once everyone was back inside.

This incident was one of the more bizarre ones that occurred during the case. To an outsider, it may sound as if someone must really have been hiding in the brush and throwing the stones. But this thinking just doesn't hold up very well, as I learned when I examined the area for myself. It turned out that the clump of brush actually grew out of a small knoll above the little trail Rick's uncle was following. I conducted several experiments there and was able to determine that rocks could not be thrown *through* the brush. You had to stand up and throw the rocks *over* the brush. Since both Rick and his uncle were focusing their flashlights on the brush, they certainly could have seen anyone cavorting about in this way. In other words, the culprit would certainly have been spotted if he had had to *stand* to throw the rocks. The fact that no one was seen indicates, at least to me, that there was no human agent involved. (It was only later that I learned about another rock-throwing case featuring a similar incident. In that case, the poltergeist was pelting a mountain cabin in Big Bear, California. When a resident of this house explored the brush near the cabin one night, rocks were thrown at her as though attracted by the glare of the flashlight.)

This singularly nasty incident on the Berkbigler property sparked off a series of more personally vindictive displays by the rock thrower. A TV crew arrived on the site on December 3 to film a story on the occurrences, and even they were pelted by the rocks. This renewed attack prompted the Berkbiglers to call the sheriffs once again. They arrived as soon as they could, but ended up suffering the brunt of the attack. One deputy was struck in broad daylight as he and Richard Berkbigler searched the brushy hill immediately behind the house. The sheriffs left the scene at 5:00 P.M., and the rock thrower pelted the house for the next three straight hours.

If all this weren't enough, an incident that occurred on Sunday, December 4, convinced the Berkbiglers that their prankster must truly be mentally deranged. Their married daughter, her husband Tim, and their twenty-one-month-old daughter arrived for a visit that morning. Tim and the little girl were playing outside on the dirt lot at about 11:30 A.M. when the daily rock-throwing began. The focus of Tim's fun was a three-wheeler motorcycle that belonged to David, which he was using to drive his daughter about. No sooner had he placed her back on the ground than a rock came flying out of nowhere and struck the little girl on the arm. Luckily, she wasn't injured, but she was badly frightened and the Berkbiglers were outraged. They immediately called the sheriff's department, which dispatched several men and a helicopter to the property in their most massive search effort yet. They combed the area for a considerable period of time, but finally had to give up.

The events of that Sunday seemed to herald the beginning of the stone thrower's most severe attack ever. By the next morning, news about the Berkbiglers' problem was being reported in the local press. That afternoon, two staff members from the *Arizona Daily Star* visited the house to write up a feature story. Carmen Duarte, a staff writer, and photographer Benjie Sanders didn't realize that they would soon become one of the phantom's targets. They arrived innocently enough at 3:45 in the afternoon when all was still quiet at the house. Mr. and Mrs. Berkbigler weren't home yet, and Rick and his younger brother Jerry, who had only recently moved back to the house, were patrolling the property. I was able to interview Ms. Duarte myself about the activity later during my investigation.

"At about 5:50 we went inside after Rick and Jerry told us that it was about time [for the rocks to start]," Ms. Duarte told me as we talked at her office. "So we went inside and when we were in, a rock hit the side door.* It was real forceful and hit real hard. Jerry and Rick were waiting for their parents and David to come home."

The Berkbiglers arrived home at 6:10 in separate cars, and their arrival seemed to aggravate the stone thrower.

---

*This refers to an entry door leading from the garage into the living room, which was a favorite target of the rock thrower.

"Rick and Jerry went out with shields and helmets to escort their parents into the house with David," the reporter continued. "Richard, the father, pulled up first, and a second later Mary and David pulled up in the van. They all came in and Richard had his jacket over his head as he entered, while Mary and David were scurrying in. We greeted each other, and after that three rocks went off while we were all in the house. They hit on the door and we could hear them hitting the cars outside. You could hear the sound of glass and the steel of the car."

The reporters were unnerved by the sound of the rocks, which were obviously quite large. They could also see the looks of anger and frustration crossing the faces of the Berkbiglers, so Ms. Duarte tried to divert their attention by proceeding with her interview.

"The stones had stopped," she went on as she reconstructed the events of that night. "He'd throw and then stop; then throw and stop. It was continuous for two whole hours. All the time we were pinned in because we didn't know when he would start throwing again. One time somebody opened the door and peeked out and a stone hit [by the door]. We say we were trapped because for the two hours we were there, stones were being thrown from 5:50 to 7:45 when the sheriffs came to escort us out. When the deputy arrived, he was hit by a stone while coming up to the house."

The Berkbiglers had called the sheriff's department a little after 7:00 P.M. to help the trapped newsreporters; but they weren't the only victims that night.

A friend of Rick's who worked for a private investigations firm had been staking out the house all day, unbeknownst to the family. The young man (who has asked that he remain anonymous because of the nature of his occupation) thought that he had a better chance of catching the culprit by working independently. That night he, too, could hear the rocks striking the house while he maintained his post in the desert. So during the siege, he quietly crept up the dirt path leading from the road to the dirt lot, silently walking his motorcycle. He couldn't see anyone near the house, but he, too, was struck in the head by a rock as he approached the garage. Luckily, he was wearing his helmet at the time, but he quickly scuttled into the house nonetheless. He left when the sheriffs arrived, only to find that his motorcycle had been struck and damaged by two more rocks.

The truly bizarre aspect of the whole series of incidents, as I learned later when I tried to reconstruct it on the site, was that visual access to the garage from the desert is obstructed by a tool shed. This shed would interfere with just about any stone thrown from the brush at the entry door, which is located on the garage's inner north wall. The entry door itself was further obstructed that night by the family van, which had been parked just in front of the open garage. There was actually only one spot on the property from which rocks could be thrown against the entry door, and that spot was in front of the brush, directly between the garage and the shed. (Stones couldn't be thrown through the brush because it was too high and thick.) Yet this area was in clear view of the house, and even illuminated by any lights left on in the living room. Both the deputies and the young investigator should have seen anyone throwing rocks at them and the door when they arrived . . . had there really been a prowler stalking them.

Another mystery was presented by the way in which the rocks invariably struck the door so repeatedly. The family's van was parked that night halfway into the garage. There was only a two-foot clearance between the roof of the vehicle and the garage opening. The doorway leading to the living room was only barely discernible, and lights were turned off in the garage once the stones started arriving. This would indicate that our hypothetical "stone thrower" was talented enough to throw a series of rocks from several yards away through a two-foot space, and strike an almost invisible target time and time again! I simply did not believe this was possible for a human prankster . . . but it *was* within the capabilities of the poltergeist.

The case was sounding stranger and stranger.

I must admit that, at first, my own feelings about the case were mixed. The area surrounding the house was so brushy that anyone could easily hide there and wouldn't have much difficulty dodging the police's surveillance. And perhaps my initial misgivings were due partly to the fact that no one with whom I spoke ever suspected a supernatural cause to the rock-throwings. But as I listened to more and more testimony, my opinion gradually changed and I found myself—almost reluctantly—coming to the conclusion that I was up against a genuine rock-throwing poltergeist. Some of the telltale features of the typical rock-throwing poltergeist were, admittedly, not present in this case. No one had seen the rocks following bizarre trajectories, making weird turns in midair, or suddenly dropping to the ground while still in flight as though striking an invisible wall. Nor did the family find the rocks unusually warm to the touch when they were retrieved. But despite the apparent "normalcy" of the rock-throwings, there were several features that precisely fit the pattern of the usual poltergeist.

It was certainly suspicious that the rocks only arrived when two or more of the family members were home. The rocks did not pelt the house when workers or the maid/cook were there alone. So the rocks were obviously focusing directly on the Berkbiglers. It was also strange that rocks would cease falling *immediately* when the family went to sleep. Rick even told me that they would retire just to stop the rock attacks. As I pointed out in the previous chapter, poltergeists seldom act up once the primary agent(s) goes to sleep. This case was definitely fitting the pattern—and I could think of no reason why a human being would cease his shenanigans just because his victims were retiring. Some of the witnesses also suggested that perhaps the rocks were being thrown by angry desert ecologists who didn't want the environment ruined by new construction. This didn't strike me as plausible because there were two other homes in the area, and neither was reporting any peltings.

I was also intrigued by what I learned about the attack on the Berkbigler's little granddaughter. When I talked to the girl's parents, it became clear that the rock that struck her was fairly large. So why wasn't she injured by it? The rock was apparently thrown from several yards away, and would have hit the girl at full force. A rock that large should have resulted in a severe trauma, but it caused far more fright than injury. This, too, is a typical pattern of the poltergeist. The historical literature is filled with cases of people who were struck by psychokinetically thrown missiles that did them no harm upon impact. Usually the amazed witnesses will see the missiles bounce off them harmlessly. It is true that Rick's uncle had been knocked unconscious by the rock-throwings, but this more recent incident with the child was right in keeping with the poltergeist's more typical habits.

There was also an added feature to the case that intrigued me. To all appearances this case seemed to represent a "pure" stone-throwing poltergeist, since no other psychokinetic disturbances were apparent. I was surprised, then, when Rick finally admitted to me that the rock-throwings were not the *only* mysterious incidents he and the others had noted during the first weeks of the case. Rick (and later Mr. Berkbigler) told me that, during the first week of the disturbances, loud knocks often sounded on the entryway door! They merely assumed that their desert-dwelling culprit was being bold and trying to frighten them. But they were puzzled that they never heard anyone approaching (or running away from) the door when the knockings came. They would rush out as soon as they heard them, but they never saw anyone high-tailing it into the desert. Rick and David also complained that "someone" would approach their windows at night and tap on them repeatedly. These are, of course, typical poltergeist tricks, though no one in the family seemed to link them with anything paranormal.*

By the end of my first day at the house, I considered it probable that I was on the track of a genuine rock-throwing poltergeist. As I probed into the case and the testimony became more and more impressive, I was eager to confront the poltergeist myself. I didn't have long to wait.

My own introduction to the Tucson rock-throwing phantom came the very night of my arrival on December 6. Since I arrived early, I was able to inspect the area, the damage caused by the rocks, piece together the history of the case, and talk with the various family members as they came home. I was even able to make a good-natured bet with one of the trackers, Mr. Kini Rae,

---

*Rick claimed that he saw a prowler looking at him through his window on one occasion during the first weeks of the rock-throwings. He only got a fleeting look at him, and I was not convinced that the figure was anything more than a trick of Rick's imagination.

that he would be unable to catch the "prankster." By this time I heartily suspected that the Berkbiglers were up against a rock-throwing poltergeist, and I was pretty sure that Kini would be stuck taking me to dinner.

When dusk finally settled over the desert, there were about fifteen to twenty people at the house. The small mob included news reporters, friends and relatives of the Berkbiglers, and the two professional trackers. Everyone was hoping that they would catch the rock thrower if he decided to show up that night. Everyone was convinced that they were up against an eccentric desert dweller or survivalist, and my presence as a parapsychologist was tolerated good-humoredly. Things began to get a little frightening, though, when some of the volunteers started showing up with rifles. Even the normally calm and collected Berkbiglers were unnerved when a crazed Vietnam veteran showed up half-drunk with his crossbow! Each volunteer or group left to stand vigil in the desert shortly after arriving, while I remained near the house and garage. I figured this was the best place to actually witness the arrival of the rocks. I wasn't too heartened, though, when I saw just how dark the desert could be at night. There was probably no more than five feet of visibility regardless of which direction you looked.

There were about six or seven of us milling around the garage when the first rock struck. I was looking out over what little landscape I could see when we all heard a rock noisily strike one of the parked cars in the dirt clearing. We could hear it bang. It was 7:03. A nervous reporter ran into the garage from the lot, and told us that he had been standing by his car, which was the automobile that had been hit. Only a couple of minutes passed before the second stone arrived. This time again, everybody near the garage could hear it strike the top of the car, roll down its side, and bump onto the ground. Everyone expected more stones to follow, but silence suddenly reigned over the desert and most of us went inside. The only exception was Kini Rae—one of the trackers—who was now more intent than ever on finding the culprit. He told me that after years of tracking animals, he liked the challenge of stalking a man. He quickly walked down the lot, making his way to the asphalt road that leads into the Berkbiglers' property. David Berkbigler joined him . . . though only after fitting himself with his trusty helmet.

Mr. Rae and David returned to the house within fifteen minutes, empty-handed. But they were now a little less sure of themselves. The twenty-three-year-old tracker from Wyoming was visibly shaken as he took me aside to tell me about the episode he and David had just experienced, which had convinced him to give up his search.

Kini related how the two of them were making their way on the road in the dark without the aid of a flashlight. Visibility was virtually nil, and although the two adventurers hadn't heard or seen the rocks thrown, they certainly felt them. Kini told me that they were walking side by side when he felt a rock gently strike him on the back. He responded immediately by pulling David to the side of the road, where they squatted down in a crouch. His reaction was almost spontaneous, and within a second or two of the rock's impact. But within only a few more seconds, another rock arrived—this one striking David in the head.

"I want to know what you think this is all about," he asked me cautiously as he concluded his story. I could do nothing but remind him about what I had said concerning poltergeists when I first arrived that afternoon.

"There's nothing normal about these rock-throwings," he said to me as he prepared to leave the house along with his sidekick. He left moments later and I never did get that free dinner in Tucson.

What so spooked Kini and fascinated me was the accuracy of the stone-throws. As a tracker used to working in the dead of night, Kini knew that you can't throw a missile in pitchblack visibility and expect to strike anything you are aiming at. Even if the first rock had been a lucky hit, any idea that they were normally propelled was extinguished by the second rock's uncanny accuracy. Experiments I conducted at the house during my visit demonstrated that a human target could only be seen from a distance *within* five or six feet. The darkness of the desert at night was so enveloping that anyone standing more than six feet away was virtually invisible. So either we were up against a poltergeist or our phantom culprit was armed with an expensive infra-red scope! This was a rather ridiculous assumption since it would be impossible to hold the scope to the eyes and at the same time throw rocks with any accuracy.

It was apparent by now that the Berkbiglers' phantom visitor wasn't about to be put off by the number of people at the house that night. David was animatedly telling everyone still inside about his adventure, and this prompted several of the family members to tell me that both David and Mr. Berkbigler were special favorites of the stone thrower. They had both been struck more often than anyone else in the family. The reporters and I were especially intrigued by this revelation, and even more when the Berkbiglers' son-in-law explained that the rock-throws would intensify if David or his father called names at the prankster. This was the first hint that this case, like so many others, actually focused on someone in the family. It was an observation we couldn't overlook, so a group of us took David outside and asked him to try. David cooperated by walking out to the middle of the lot and proceeded to yell at the stone thrower. His invectives included a number of colorful remarks disdaining the prankster's possible race and sexual preference.

David continued the name-calling for a minute or two. There was no immediate response, so he started back to the garage.

"See, he doesn't hate me more than anyone else," he said as he approached us. But no sooner were these words out of his mouth than a large rock came flying out of the desert. It struck noisily inside the garage where it hit the south wall—with such force that everyone went scurrying into the house for cover.

I alone stood my ground. I wanted to retrieve the rock to see if it was hot, a phenomenon often reported in such cases. I also wanted to mark the rock to see if it would be rethrown at us if I pitched it back into the desert. This, too, is a favorite trick of the rock-throwing poltergeist. The desert night got the better of me, though, and I wasn't able to find the missile.

The little experiment we had just conducted was so intriguing that I soon gave up my search to see if I could convince David to repeat it. He was in the house talking to his parents at this time, so I gathered them together and explained what I wanted to do.

Mr. and Mrs. Berkbigler were a little apprehensive, since they certainly didn't want their son used as bait, but I assured them that I would station him in a safe place, and would even shield him myself. The Berkbiglers finally agreed after making sure David still had his helmet handy, and I took him outside once again. This time I asked him to crouch down next to the family's van, which had been parked in the middle of the dirt lot. I stood right next to him, and draped myself over him for added protection, before urging him to begin yelling at the stone thrower. He was asking me what he should yell when both of us heard a large rock fall directly behind us. It sounded as if it had simply been dropped, almost playfully, to startle us; it didn't strike and roll as if it had been thrown. No further rocks arrived despite David's subsequent cajoling, and we reluctantly returned to the house.

It was well past 8:00 P.M. by now, and the weary vigilantes were all coming in from the field rather discouraged. No one had been seen throwing rocks, so everyone congregated in the living room to discuss the best way to catch the prowler. Some of the volunteers wanted to organize into search teams, while yet others preferred working solo. Some of the Vietnam veterans offered suggestions they had picked up during their experiences at jungle warfare. It seemed that everyone had a plan, and Mr. Berkbigler took it all in with good humor. I could tell that he was pleased that at least now he could count on someone to help him, even though the volunteers were doing little better than the sheriffs had done during their searches. The conversation became rather heated, and finally the Berkbiglers' son-in-law left the house. Several more minutes passed before we all heard a rock strike the entry door. The sound was unmistakable and rather startling, since it was thrown forcefully. Tim came running back a second later, excitedly announcing that the stone thrower had tried to pick him off as he approached the entry.

"That's him all right," exclaimed Mr. Berkbigler. "He always throws one last rock at the door, just to let us know he's still out there."

Richard Berkbigler was correct, since no further rocks were thrown that evening. The poltergeist was retiring for the night, to everyone's relief but—in a way—regret. Mr. Berkbigler was battle-weary, the volunteers were frustrated, his sons were angry, and I was fascinated. I had been especially impressed by how the rocks were being thrown in the dark with such accuracy. Even Mr. Berkbigler finally had to agree that the "prankster" was not only sly and desert-wise, but also uncannily accurate. The flying rocks that night did not unequivocally prove to me that a poltergeist was loose on his property, and the "human agency" theory was at least *reasonably* possible. But the accuracy of the stone-throws kept me betting on the side of the poltergeist. The fact that they were now apparently focusing on David and his father perhaps indicated that the rock-throwings were about to take on an ever-more characteristic (poltergeistlike) appearance.

The poltergeist's early retirement also allowed me to begin making psychological and neurological assessments of the various family members. This is part and parcel of any proper investigation of a probable poltergeist case. I began my work a bit skeptically, though. When you have been on a number of these investigations, it generally isn't hard to tell when you are dealing with a typical poltergeist family. These families are usually disturbed and dysfunctional. They tend to repress their feelings and stifle their emotions. The poor family that suffered the object-throwing poltergeist I recounted in Chapter 2 is fairly typical of what you run into. This is why poltergeist investigations can be so disheartening. Although you sometimes get to witness the displays at first hand, you also see an enormous amount of human suffering. Poltergeist investigations just aren't very pretty affairs.

But this family was breaking all the rules! I didn't see a single hint of pathology during my first day with them. There were the usual tensions and parent/child annoyances seen in any family, but to all appearances the Berkbiglers were a typical middle-class, all-American, and very loving family. I was continually impressed during my stay by how well-balanced every member of the family seemed to be. They certainly didn't seem repressed about their emotions, and they were all intelligent people. If somehow this family was unleashing the poltergeist, the dynamics behind the attack were awfully subtle.

It was in order to better understand the family interactions that I began my work that night. I gave several of them two questionnaires. The first was the Minnesota Multiphasic Personality Inventory, which gauges several personality characteristics, such as tendencies toward a variety of mental problems. I also gave them a questionnaire designed to isolate any neurological problems they might be suffering. It was here that I accidentally stumbled onto the possible cause of the outbreak. Based on their responses to the questions, it didn't strike me that either Mr. Berkbigler or his sons, Jerry and Rick, were suffering any neurological problems. But when it came to David, there were indications of an undiagnosed symptom. In response to one of my questions, David explained to me that he often smelled foul odors, like excrement. He usually experienced the sensation about twice a week, and it didn't matter where he was. The odors would come whether he was at work or recreation. I spoke about David's complaint to his father, who admitted that David often complained about the odors to him. He tended to dismiss the incidents as a result of his son's imagination. But to anyone trained in neurology, David's complaint was more than revealing. His olfactory hallucination was probably indicating that he suffered from anomalous electrical activity in the temporal lobes of his brain. Spontaneous neural activity in that location causes a variety of hallucinatory experiences, the most common being the odor of either burning or rotting food, or excrement.

This was the kind of clue I was looking for as I interviewed the family, since poltergeist activity is sometimes linked to brain dysfunctions. David's complaint, and the condition it might be indicating, were both harmless enough. It didn't seem that he was suffering from full-blown temporal lobe epilepsy, only that there was abnormal neuronal "firing" in his brain. This was not a long-standing condition with David either, since the olfactory hallucinations began only two weeks prior to my investigation.

I explained all of my thoughts to Mr. Berkbigler later that night. He listened sympathetically and never once chided me for my belief in the paranormal. But, he said, he was sure that the rocks were being thrown by a human hand. We would have to wait for the next night, he added, to catch the psychopath.

The next night finished up even more dramatically, but once again it was hard to determine the cause of the rock-throws. Because several newspapers and TV stations in the area were running stories on the case, there was a mass of people at the house by the time the sun set. The crowd included volunteers, news teams, sheriffs, and several just-plain curiosity seekers. The Berkbiglers were welcoming everyone to the house who wanted to help find the prankster, and one enterprising teenager even showed up with a floodlight he wanted to install on the roof. The crowd rather annoyed the sheriffs, who repeatedly requested Mr. Berkbigler to ask them all to leave. But by this time, the trucker felt his friends could do a better job than the deputies and refused to call the volunteers in from the field. The sheriffs left that evening before any stones were thrown, complaining that the family was making it impossible for them to do their job. Everyone else faded into the desert as darkness swept over the area.

There were only a few stones thrown that (Wednesday) night. The first struck at 6:39 and plowed into the little toolshed, scaring the dickens out of a *Tucson Citizen* reporter who was hiding there.

Douglas Kreutz recounted the incident himself in the next day's edition of the paper:

> To observe last evening's rock bombardment at the far Northeast Side home of Richard and Mary Berkbigler, I selected a spot in a little tool shed 10 yards southwest of the house.
>
> The shed seemed like a pretty safe place to be when the rocks began to fly. The roof and walls were made of a good, solid corrugated material, and I had pulled a piece of good, solid plywood across the door opening. The piece of plywood, somewhat smaller than the door opening, would provide adequate protection from flying stones while allowing me an unobstructed view of the house and driveway.
>
> At 6:39 P.M., the evening's first rock crashed into the east wall of the shed.
>
> The rock made quite a noise and startled me. But it didn't enter the shed, and I felt content with my choice of shelter.

But on this evening the rocks seemed to be focusing their fury on the dirt path leading from the road up to the Berkbiglers' lot. Two independent news reporters were walking up the path when a rock grazed the head of one of them. But the most impressive incident of the night occurred at 7:30 along the same path.

Five local teenagers were coming up the path when the rock thrower struck. The boys told me later that they were walking almost side-by-side when one of them, fifteen-year-old Jeff Cook, was picked off by a rock. It was very dark on the path, and Jeff explained that he was a little behind the others when the rock smacked right into his neck under his jaw line. The force was so great that it stunned him, but it didn't cause him any injury. It didn't appear to me that the teenager was lying, since he was sporting a three-inch red mark on his neck where the stone had struck. It was a rather nasty-looking mark, and indicated that the rock must have been over three inches long. But what was truly bizarre about the whole incident was that the rock had not caused the young man any serious injury. A rock that size, thrown from any distance, could have broken his jaw or bruised him severely. I kept tabs on Jeff for the rest of the night and was surprised when the mark on his jaw didn't swell. I spoke to him the next day when he visited the house again, and saw that the red mark had not even turned black and blue. So the stone must have struck Jeff with less force than it should have under normal conditions.

(Note once again that this just happens to be one of the most famous trademarks of the rock-throwing poltergeist.)

I was still talking with the boys when the real excitement of the evening got under way. Rick came bursting into the house right before 8:00 P.M., quickly announcing to everyone that he had caught sight of the culprit! He explained how he was patrolling the south side of the house when he nearly tripped over a mysterious stranger hiding near some bushes. The man was wearing dark clothing, a black cap, and gloves, and had fled after being detected. Rick was annoyed by the encounter since he was sure he could have caught the man . . . had he not had to tangle with an unfriendly cactus when setting off in pursuit. Several volunteers were still at the house when Rick was telling his story, so just about everyone rushed out with him to search the back hill toward which the culprit had run. I stayed behind, and the reporters present and I could hear their calls and the crunching sound of their movements from the hill. The noise was not loud enough, however, to drown out the sound of another rock striking outside in front of the house minutes later. It was certainly clear that *this* rock was not being thrown by the man being chased.

Only a few more minutes passed before the young man on the roof called out. He had located the prowler on the hill with his floodlight. It now looked as though the mysterious stranger was about to be caught, but then the floodlight malfunctioned. The hill was once again shrouded in darkness, and the prowler was able to make his getaway.

Mr. Berkbigler, however, was encouraged by the near miss. When he returned to the house with several of the volunteers, he sat down on the couch and suggested that perhaps they had scared away the prowler once and for all.

He also smiled at me for a moment. "What do you think of your theory now?" he scoffed good-naturedly about my poltergeist hunting. I could do little but grin back.

I had to admit that poltergeists don't take the form of prowlers wearing caps and gloves. The night's activities, I told him openly, constituted the first hard evidence that perhaps the rock-throwings had a human cause. What I didn't tell my host was that I was still skeptical that this "prowler" was also the stone thrower. My skepticism was increased by the fact that the man had been isolated on the back hill only two minutes after I heard a rock strike in front of the house. My guess was that the man was either a volunteer who had come to the house unbeknownst to the family, or perhaps even a deputy left by the sheriff to keep an eye on things. Despite my unspoken misgivings, Mr. Berkbigler was more convinced than ever that the mystery prowler was the stone thrower when no rocks hit the house the next night. His prediction bore out, for December 7 represented the last night that the phantom stone thrower manifested.

Poltergeist or prowler? It was hard for me to tell as I got ready to catch my flight back to Los Angeles that Friday. Everything pointed to a poltergeist, in my opinion, except for the identity of the mysterious stranger spotted on Wednesday. I was pondering this very issue when I decided to call in at the sheriff's substation near the Berkbiglers' home before boarding my plane. I needed to make the call since the local sheriffs had agreed to provide me with some of their own information on the Berkbiglers' problem. I spoke with the deputy now in charge of the case and was somewhat surprised when he asked me what *I* thought the cause was. I explained that there was evidence for both the poltergeist theory and the prankster theory and, at the deputy's request, I started listing the relative arguments for both possibilities. I was just starting to tell him about Wednesday night's prowler when he interrupted me, saying that his department knew the identity of the prowler. This surprised me no end, so I tried getting more information from the deputy, who further advised me that the man had nothing to do with the stone-throwings. These hints made it quite clear that the prowler *had* been a deputy left on the property to keep an eye on things, as I had suspected. I tried to get the deputy to tell me who the man was, but he kept begging off for "security" reasons. I am sure he didn't want it known that he was hiding men on the Berkbiglers' property, nor was I baffled by why the officer had run after being spotted. You don't hold your ground and try to identify yourself when twenty angry people are running at you with clubs, baseball bats, and rocks!

By the time I boarded my plane, I was once again fairly convinced that I had been witness to the handiwork of a rock-throwing poltergeist. Everything I had seen and heard fitted the pattern of these mysterious psychic visitors. In fact, this mysterious episode of paranormal rock throwing *followed every single pattern of the stone-throwing poltergeist:*

1. The attacks began suddenly and ceased just as mysteriously three months later.
2. The stones showered down only when the Berkbiglers were home, and even focused their fury on two specific members of the family.
3. The rocks, although thrown from the pitchblack desert, arrived with uncanny accuracy. The aim of the rock thrower seemed supernormally accurate.

4. Despite the presence of sheriffs, helicopters, and up to twenty volunteers on occasion, no one ever caught or even saw any prankster throwing the rocks. The rocks kept coming even during the searches.

5. Even large rocks (usually) didn't hurt anyone, even when they struck forcefully. This is a dead giveaway and conforms to many historical stone-throwing poltergeist cases. Back in the 1650s, for instance, one witness to such a poltergeist wrote that ". . . stones were thrown at those that were present, which hit them, but hurt them not."

6. Some of the family members observed a series of rocks flying out of a bush when it could be clearly seen that no one was near it.

Shortly before leaving town I also discovered that the local sheriffs were beginning to take the poltergeist theory more seriously than ever before. When I spoke to the detective in charge, I learned that he was gathering information on a similar rock-throwing case reported from Big Bear, California, in 1962.

Any lingering trepidations I may have had about the case were not appreciated by the Berkbiglers. They were just happy that the whole affair was finally over. Now they could get back to finishing their lovely desert home . . . and living there in peace. But I was still left with a most annoying question in my mind. Why had this well-knit and mutually supportive family suddenly been the focus of a poltergeist attack? My answer then was the same as it is now: I don't really know. But I believe that it may very well relate to neurological effects inside fifteen-year-old David's brain. Temporal-lobe problems in boys his age are very rare. It seems more than suspicious that the Berkbiglers would find themselves up against *two* unlikely events (the poltergeist and a son with this rare condition) unless they were connected.

The case also fitted yet another pattern. For as I will show at the end of this book, there is growing evidence that poltergeist agents suffer all sorts of eruptions in their central nervous systems, including epilepsy. So if David wasn't a poltergeist agent in more typical respects, there was neurological evidence that he fit other patterns we are now associating with this great (and bothersome!) visitor from the unknown.

Part 2

Poltergeists, Hauntings, and the Mind

6

Three Poltergeist Hauntings

Poltergeists are phenomenologically related to hauntings and haunted houses in general. Both types of paranormal infestation share many common features. Both involve houses where seemingly inexplicable events are recurrently transpiring.

Despite the fact that ghostly sights and sounds will break out in both hauntings and poltergeists, these two phenomena still tend to represent fairly distinct syndromes. By tradition, hauntings focus on a house and do not specifically center on anyone living there. They do not "focus" on a living person the way poltergeists usually do; they seem to be independent of those fortunate enough to witness them. It is therefore not unusual for several successive families to encounter psychic events while living in one of these plagued abodes. The general rule is that while poltergeists infest a *person,* a haunting infests a *place.* Poltergeists tend to come fast and furious before burning out, but hauntings can be more subtle and often display considerable longevity. Some may go on for well over a hundred years.

Even the effects produced by poltergeists and hauntings often differ. From the previous chapters you should have a good idea of the type and range of phenomena a poltergeist can pro-

duce. The most apt description I can think of for the activities of
the poltergeist would be *dynamic*. There is a certain, almost frantic, dynamism that underlies the typical poltergeist. Hauntings,
on the other hand, seem to be more "laid back." Violent psychokinetic disturbances rarely occur, since hauntings tend to rely
more on producing eerie sights and sounds, such as apparitions
or the sound of mysterious footsteps. Hauntings just don't seem
to have the raw energy that animates the poltergeist.

To give you a better idea of the dynamics of a typical haunting, the following two case reports should be examined. The first
was sent to me by a woman currently living in a so-called
"haunted house." She wrote to me hoping that I could proffer an
explanation for the strange occurrences she was witnessing:

> On Sept. 19, 1969, we spent our first night in the
> house. I was sleeping in the front bedroom with my two
> younger sisters. I awoke at dawn. I looked through the door-
> way into the kitchen, and saw all the pots and pans "float-
> ing" around the kitchen. I was almost nine years old at the
> time. I thought that someone was playing a trick on me by
> using strings and was up in the attic. I went into the kitchen
> to see if there were strings attached to the pots and pans. I
> found none. I was so scared that I went back to bed and
> pulled the covers over my head.

> The next experience was about three years later. My
> mother, brother, sisters and I had been to the movies. My
> father was home asleep. My sister and I were the first ones
> in the house. Dad got up and asked us why we had come into
> the house and gone back out about ten minutes earlier. We
> had not. My father said that he heard the front door unlock
> and open and close, and then someone walking through the
> living room and kitchen. "It" went down the hallway, un-
> locked the inside back door, went out, and then unlocked the
> outside back door. Then "it" came back in, locking doors
> behind "it," went back through the hallway, kitchen and
> living room, cursing the whole way and slamming the front
> door.

> The regular occurrences started within the next few
> months.

At night we would hear someone standing by the beds and breathing hard. My mother and I were the main ones to hear this. My sister did not hear it for several years.

At this time my father worked away from home and was only home on weekends. My mother got into the habit of staying up late at night, watching TV and knitting or doing embroidery. A rocking chair in the living room would rock almost every night as if someone was keeping her company.

At this point we started calling the ghost "Hans." The reason for this was because my mother believed the ghost to be a poltergeist (the German word for ghost) so we gave him a German name.

"Hans" started doing all kinds of things including breathing heavily by the beds, turning lights on and off, and we could hear footsteps around the house. The only room in the house where we never heard or saw anything was the bathroom. All the other rooms were fair game.

Every night we heard Hans breathing by the beds. The first night that my father heard "Hans" turned out to be rather funny. Father always kept a pistol and bullets with him in his suitcase. One weekend when he was home, he heard "Hans" breathing by the foot of the bed. He thought that it was a real person. He got out of the bed, waking Mom up in the process, to get his pistol and shoot whoever was there. It took Mom about 20 minutes to convince him that it was "Hans."

The summer of 1974 "Hans" was very busy. One night a girl was staying with us. During the night Mom and Dad heard a voice from outside their room saying, "I have had it. I'm leaving here." Then they heard someone slamming the front door on the way out. They (my parents) thought the girl staying with us had left. They went outside looking for her but could not find her, so Mom decided to check her bed. There she was, sound asleep. My folks decided "Hans" had gotten into an argument with someone.

"Hans" had a nightly pattern he went through in the bedroom my sister and I slept in. At about 2:00 A.M. every morning he would walk into the room, then wait a few seconds and drop something heavy on the floor. I always woke up and heard him go through this for about two years, although I never saw him. I just heard his footsteps in the room and then the heavy thud on the floor.

The family was eventually able to trace what they felt to be the cause of the disturbance. This is very typical of the sort of causation that traditionally gives rise to these unusual events.

As my correspondent continued:

> My great-grandfather had killed himself in this room in 1962. He had shot himself. Everyone in the family knew this, but in 1976 only one living person knew where his body was found. That was my great-grandmother, his wife. The thought finally dawned on me that he was reliving his death. We were hearing all the sounds except the gunshot. I got my great-grandmother into the room and asked her if the spot where I heard the heavy thud was where she had found great-grandfather. She went white as a sheet and asked my father to take her home. From then on I never heard him do it again.
>
> He started doing other things. Some nights I would hear the sound of his cane tapping on the floor and his wheelchair rolling around.

A similar case was brought to my attention in 1981. This case was reported from a large city in the Midwest. One of the residents living in the house originally contacted me because she was so frightened by what was occurring there. She was living there with her daughter, her brothers, and their parents.

This case differs from the previous one since apparitions actually were seen. Despite this element in the report, the witnesses were never able to come up with a solution to the haunting. The events long remained just a series of strange and inexplicable occurrences. Part of my correspondent's account reads:

> One night, at about 1:00 A.M., my daughter and I were home while my parents and older brother were on vacation,

and the other brother was out of the house; we settled down to go to sleep. My oldest daughter was sleeping on the sofa that night and I was sleeping in the downstairs front bedroom that belongs to my parents. I was just about to drop off to sleep when I heard footsteps walking overhead in my vacationing brother's bedroom. I asked my oldest daughter if my brother Joe had come in while I was in the shower and she said, "No. Why?" I told her I heard footsteps in my [other] brother John's room. She said, "Yeah, sure." The footsteps started at the west side of the house and continued east without stop. There is a wall dividing the two bedrooms and these footsteps did not stop at the wall or go out into the hallway to continue their tread. My oldest daughter heard them over her head and dove into bed with me and my youngest daughter. My mother has heard these footsteps when everyone is in bed as well as the sound of furniture being moved when there is no one but her, she and I, or my father and her in the house. We've smelled perfume, heard someone laughing, crying, talking, and even seen mists in the bedrooms upstairs. My parents refuse to believe that we have all heard *something* while lying in bed at night, unable to sleep.

They've yelled upstairs at us many times to get out of my brothers' bedrooms and for the boys to go to bed when, in fact, they were either not home, or in bed sound asleep. Most nights, we lock our aged German shepherd dog in the kitchen, but on nights when the footsteps make their way across the second floor of our house, he cries. I have never made the association that his whining foretells our visitor's walk before. But as of Sept. 2, 1981, I no longer doubt the dog's ability to sense a ghost or a nightly visitor who isn't there.

My mother and I have heard furniture move upstairs when we both know no one but we two are home and I invariably got sent upstairs to investigate. Nothing has been touched, no beds out of place, no one home up there but my older brother's goldfish—and they don't walk!

I myself have had an "encounter" some time ago where I smelled violets or some other sweet-smelling flower scent in the bedroom that is now my brother's room. It was the middle of summer. I was sound asleep and no air conditioner was running. I felt a cold draft, smelled this sweet fragrance, opened my eyes, and saw the corner of the mattress I was lying on indent like someone just sat on it and there was no one there.

On Christmas Day, 1980, my younger brother saw a blonde girl in a yellow summer dress standing by his closet door. My daughter was trying to wake him at the time. He accused her of spraying his room with lilac perfume. My daughter wears no such scent nor do any of the women in our house wear such a flowery fragrance.

My oldest daughter says she saw a young girl sitting on her dresser one night when some deflated balloons she had tacked to her bedroom wall fell on her face while she was sleeping. We then found rose petals in her room when we have never had flowers (even plastic) up in that one particular room. My other brother has smelled some kind of perfume in his room at night, too. He tried to blame my daughters and me but we don't wear perfume except on special occasions. He claims his room is always cold at night even during the summer. He always sleeps with a heavy sleeping bag (opened up) on his bed, and says it's the ghost that plays these tricks on us. Some nights we'd all be asleep and I would hear him complain to someone to get out of his room and let him sleep.

I pointed out at the beginning of this chapter that the characteristics differentiating hauntings from poltergeists are traditional ones. They are only general guidelines, and certainly do not represent absolutes. So I would now like to introduce a rather strange idea to you:

Some cases that look like traditional hauntings are nothing of the sort. They are actually disguised poltergeists being created by the people currently living in the house.

I came to this conclusion several years ago, when I first started investigating hauntings. By tradition, hauntings come into being when a tragedy or other emotional event has occurred in a given location. This event or series of events somehow impresses itself onto the "atmosphere" of the place, which then affects the people who come into contact with it. Spirits of the dead have little to do with most hauntings, since the witness is usually merely experiencing the residual emotions set up by the past tragedy. These "traces" tend to translate into apparitions, odd sounds, odors, and—on rare occasions—the paranormal movement of household objects. Now this is, of course, a very stock explanation for hauntings, but it is very true of most cases. But I also gradually learned during my years in the field that not all hauntings can be accounted for with such facility. Many times you will find yourself checking out hauntings where there is no history of tragedy associated with the residence. What do you do, for instance, when you are called in to investigate a house being infested with apparitions and mysterious footsteps . . . only to discover that it is a two-year-old tract home still owned by the couple who originally bought it? Or when you check out the history of an alleged "haunted" house and learn that not a single previous tenant ever encountered anything strange there?

These represent just the sort of cases I've come across over the years. They gradually led me to believe that some hauntings —just like poltergeists—can be generated by the living. There were actually three separate clues that led me to this position:

1. Sometimes when you investigate a haunting, you find the same kind of underlying family psychodynamics that you discover when examining poltergeists.
2. Cases that at first appear to be conventional hauntings sometimes transform into classic poltergeists when they begin to escalate.
3. People who find themselves living in a haunted house sometimes complain that they have run into similar problems all their lives.

To make these points as forceful as possible, I would now like to present three cases that tread that eerie and murky border between poltergeists and hauntings. The following cases seem to share characteristics drawn from each category. I like to call these cases *poltergeist hauntings*, since they feature the phenomenology of a haunting while exhibiting some of the psychodynamics of your typical poltergeist.

THE STRANGE CASE OF MR. AND MRS. ROSE AND THEIR ODORIFEROUS POLTERGEIST

Early in 1977 I was called in to investigate a "haunted house" in the Los Angeles suburb of Canoga Park. The family first made contact with me after reading an article about me in a local newspaper. They were hoping that I could shed some much needed light on their problem. Since my callers seemed very depressed and anxiety-ridden, I made an appointment to see them that very night.

When I arrived at their house early that evening, I could see that the family was in the throes of a major crisis. The household consisted of a middle-aged couple, whom I'll call the Roses, and their eight-year-old son. They were living in a lower-middle-class neighborhood and were obviously having a difficult time dealing with the events plaguing them. Luckily, there was one additional witness to the events, since Mrs. Rose's mother was a frequent visitor to the house and was willing to corroborate the story I was about to hear. This woman turned out to be an especially level-headed witness, and I was later to place considerable stock in her testimony.

When I first walked in the door, the Roses escorted me through their small two-bedroom house, invited me to sit down, and then told me one of the strangest stories I've ever heard.

Mr. Rose began the conversation by explaining just why he had called me. The cause of his complaint was not an unusual one. Both Mr. and Mrs. Rose claimed that their home was being attacked by eruptions of sweet-smelling odors. The odor was invariably that of violets and was almost overpowering. It would come out of nowhere, pervade the entire house, linger, and then dissipate instantaneously. Both of the Roses as well as their son (who spoke little during the interview but clung fearfully beside his mother) reported several episodes. The eruptions had been going on for several weeks, and the family was tired of them.

They wanted to know what was going on and hoped I would shed some light on the mystery.

My own reaction to the story was fairly positive. I certainly wasn't skeptical, since the overpowering smell of violets is a very common feature of some haunted houses. The same phenomenon was noted, for instance, in one of the cases I cited at the opening of this chapter. Other similar accounts have been placed in the literature as well.* Since it was clear to me that none of the family members knew very much about hauntings or poltergeists, I didn't think they were acquainted enough with the literature to "crib" the account in order to impress me.

I was wary about accepting the story at face value, though. This was why I was very impressed when Mrs. Rose's mother, who joined us that evening, added her testimony to that of her daughter and son-in-law. She explained how she had once smelled the violets while cleaning the house one afternoon. She was alone in the house cleaning the carpet near the front door when the pervading odor precipitated. The odor seemed to emanate originally from the kitchen, she explained, and then quickly permeated the entire house. It remained present for about half a minute before dissipating instantaneously.

After spending considerable time talking with the family, I came to the conclusion that we were probably not dealing with a traditional haunting. There was no history of tragedy associated with the post–World War II tract home, and the Roses—who had already lived in the house for a few years—reported no previous psychic encounters. I therefore found myself drawn to the idea that perhaps the Roses were up against a disguised poltergeist— that is, a psychic attack they were somehow producing themselves, but which was masquerading in the guise of a haunting. While I had never heard of a poltergeist case that *just* produced odors and no other sign of activity, I recalled that the strong odor of violets played a conspicuous role in at least one famous historical poltergeist. (This case was investigated and reported in 1958

---

*During the same general time I was looking into this case, my colleague Charles Moses was checking out a haunted house in another section of Los Angeles. This family, too, complained of the smell of violets in the house. Moses ultimately experienced one of these episodes himself.

by Dr. Nandor Fodor, who pioneered the psychological study of the poltergeist in his book *On the Trail of the Poltergeist.*) My suspicions encouraged me to ask the family what was going on in their lives *psychologically*. That's when I learned that the psychic outbreak they were confronting was probably an outgrowth from a great deal of pent-up and poorly expressed frustration they were experiencing. The psychic odors paled in significance when compared to the psychological nightmare the family was enduring.

Through careful questioning, I learned that Mr. Rose's extended family was prone to bickering and feuding in a most pathological way. Threats of physical violence were commonplace between warring factions within the family, and the family was currently at each other's throats once again. It was this situation that apparently led to the outbreak.

Several months before the odoriferous attacks started, Mr. Rose's mother apparently decided that her son had not been a "good enough" son to her. She made this known to the guilty man in no uncertain terms, and it didn't help when she died only a few months later. Mr. Rose was probably harboring a great deal of guilt over his mother's invectives and death. When the elderly woman died, the rest of the family went in for the attack as well; he decided that one cause of the woman's demise was the anguish she felt over her son's filial "betrayal." Mr. Rose, I might add, didn't have the slightest idea why his mother had turned on him . . . it all just seemed part of her nature.

Soon the Roses were receiving bizarre phone calls from their relatives. His brother and his family would call him even in the middle of the night, blaming him for his mother's death and threatening to put a curse on him! (These threats were doubly bizarre since Mr. Rose came from a Jewish-American family, where superstitious cultural beliefs play practically no role.) The calls were vicious, and it looked like everyone in the extended family was ganging up on the poor man.

Mr. and Mrs. Rose simply didn't have the psychological resources to handle the guilt and the pressure; this was very clear to me as they told me their sad story. Nor, apparently, did they have the fortitude to simply hang up on their relatives, or to suggest a rather hot spot where these people could vacation indefinitely. The pressure had taken its toll on the family, who felt themselves totally threatened. They couldn't get any sleep, their son was now ill with an undiagnosed and mysterious ailment, and they were terrified that the paranormal events taking place in their house would escalate. They were beginning to believe that the odoriferous attacks were the result of their relation's curse, and *that they were the victims of black magic.*

I was absolutely appalled by the story I was hearing, especially since the Roses didn't possess the necessary psychological strength to strike back at their sadistic relatives. It seemed obvious that their son's debilitating illness (which was manifesting as chronic fatigue) was also a result of psychological stress. But just what could I do? The Roses (and their relatives) needed a psychiatrist even more than they needed a parapsychologist.

My advice to the family was that they start putting up a fight against their relatives. No one should be subjected to the type of psychological abuse that they were undergoing, I added. Since I am not a licensed psychologist, I did not want to counsel the family in any further depth, but I did give them a few ideas about how they could handle the situation. It was apparent that the Roses' immediate problem was with their relatives, not with the "ghost" and its ghostly odors. Since the odors were harmless, I suggested that they simply ignore them. By this time I was quite sure that the odors, too, were being produced by the family itself as a result of their life situation, but I felt it wouldn't be wise to explain to them that they were probably causing their own problem. I merely assured them that the odors would cease when they became psychologically stronger.

This may sound like I was "playing psychiatrist." Remember, though, that I had been called in by this family to help them. My feeling was that there was nothing I could do to help them parapsychologically with their problem. Since it was clear that Mr. Rose was the product of a severely dysfunctional family, I suggested that both he and his wife (and eventually their son) get involved in a professional counseling program and learn the coping strategies they so desperately needed but had never learned in the past. I assured them over and over that when they were emotionally healthier, their haunting would simply go away.

The family was obviously puzzled by my emphasis on their domestic rather than psychic problem, and I don't think they ever realized just *what* I was getting at. But I had an ally in Mrs. Rose's mother, who immediately picked up on and understood why I was so interested in all the feuding. She constantly reinforced what I was saying, and even offered to baby-sit her grandson so that they could explore family counseling further.

When I left the house later that night, I wished the Roses good luck. I told them that they could always call me if they encountered any other difficulties in the house; but I never heard from them again.

INVESTIGATING A "TALKING" POLTERGEIST IN DOWNTOWN LOS ANGELES

I certainly had little idea what Raymond Bayless and I were up against in 1973, when we decided to investigate what sounded like a typical haunting near downtown Los Angeles. The call had originally come into the offices of the Southern California Society for Psychical Research in Beverly Hills, and the SCSPR immediately contacted us about mounting an investigation for them. The caller turned out to be a young mother whom I'll call Mrs. Helen Thomas, who was hearing voices and seeing an apparition in her home.

When we visited her a few days later, we found that Mrs. Thomas was living in a rather old and poorly maintained rented house near downtown Los Angeles. Besides conducting her drafting work from the house, the residence served as living quarters for her mother, her small daughter, and herself.

Strange events had been going on in the house for several weeks. Mrs. Thomas explained to us that she would often hear her name called out by an invisible presence. She had put down the experiences to her imagination at first. But as we munched away on cookies and coffee, she told us that her real concern came when the other members of the family began hearing the voices, too. The final straw came only a week before, she added, when her daughter asked, "Why don't you answer the man, Mommy?" This incident had caused Mrs. Thomas considerable anxiety, since she didn't want her little girl involved with whatever force was loose in the house.

Later we were able to talk to Mrs. Thomas's mother, and she too corroborated that she had heard the mysterious voice.

But this wasn't the extent of the haunting, by any means. Mrs. Thomas also told us that, on one occasion, she had seen a whitish female figure in the dining room. It seemed to resemble a human being, she said, and it dissolved as she watched it. Mrs. Thomas also claimed that on returning home from shopping or errands, she sometimes found household objects turned over mysteriously. Since the family nucleus included two dogs and a rather rambunctious cat, we preferred to believe that the pets were the gremlins responsible for at least this aspect of the haunting. This idea wasn't taken too enthusiastically by our hostess, who tended to reject our explanation.

By the end of our interview, neither Raymond nor I had formed any definite opinion about the case. We learned during our conversation that the Thomases were suffering from the abuse of an alcoholic neighbor who had maliciously thrown stones at the house in the past. It seemed reasonable to assume that perhaps he might be the culprit responsible for the mysterious events and voices. We also thought that perhaps the apparition Mrs. Thomas saw on that one occasion was the result of her overwrought imagination. So the best thing we could do was to simply counsel the family about what hauntings seem to be, to emphasize that the disturbances were harmless, and that—if nothing else—they shouldn't be frightened by them. We also emphasized that the events would probably soon abate and suggested they try to keep their minds off what was happening in the house. This is all standard advice we usually give to families who contact us when they either think or really *are* being plagued by psychic disturbances. Both Mrs. Thomas and her mother struck us as very intelligent people, though understandably frightened by the disturbances. But there really wasn't much we could do about their problem.

Our investigation of this case was fairly routine. There was little to differentiate this complaint from dozens of other calls we have received over the years. Families who find themselves the center of such psychic outbreaks usually just want to talk to someone. When this need has been fulfilled, we rarely receive follow-up calls.

But this case was destined to be different. Raymond called me two months later to say that Mrs. Thomas had just phoned him. The events at her house were picking up again, and this time they were becoming more intense. So we felt it worthwhile to pay a second visit to the Thomas family the very next day.

We found that Mrs. Thomas was still in a very anxious frame of mind. The events that had occurred the day before (and which had precipitated her call to Raymond) were still fresh in her mind. We were finally able to calm her down a bit and then learned just *what* had so frightened her. The distraught woman explained how the latest paranormal outbreak had begun the previous evening. She and her daughter were sitting in the back bedroom, the little girl watching TV and Mrs. Thomas reading on the bed.

"Around 8:30 she turned around and asked me who it was' that she heard calling me," she told us. "I told her I had heard nothing. She repeated that someone was calling me from the hall or the bathroom and I had better go check. She insisted that someone was calling my name, and that the voice was male. We went together down the hall to the area in front of the bathroom door and she said the voice was coming from there. I told her she was just hearing an echo from next door. (The neighbors fight often and are quite noisy.) We then walked into the living room and stood just inside the door."

It was at this point that the outbreak took on a new and more frightening dimension. Mrs. Thomas went on to tell us how she was standing in the living room when her mother's camera threw itself at her from a table.

"It landed at my feet and just sort of bounced," she explained. "Then the front door started slamming and the dogs started barking and crying."

This was the end of the disturbances for the moment, so Mrs. Thomas made a hasty retreat back to the bedroom. Her daughter was finally able to go to sleep, but the eruption recommenced about an hour later. The tip-off that a second psychic disturbance was brewing came when the dogs started barking again for no apparent reason. The distraught woman described the events as they had ensued:

> I went to the front of the house to check [the dogs]. The door was slamming and bouncing on its hinges. The two dogs were aimed at the door and their hair was standing straight up, while they were barking. It was a warning bark, so I opened the inside door to see who was there. The screen door just slammed in my face. I locked the inside door as fast as possible and ran like hell for the bedroom. My daughter was still asleep and had not been bothered. The dogs barked and howled three more times during the night. These times I did not check. Around 12:30 I began to hear voices just sort of discussing something out of my hearing. Again I checked, but there was nothing to be found. The house has a parking lot just outside the windows. Thinking it might have come from there, I opened all the windows to see. Nothing was in the parking lot. It sounded like a large group of people murmuring quietly just out of earshot.

The poor woman was now doubly alarmed, since she was afraid that someone might be injured by flying objects, especially her young daughter. We, on the other hand, were a bit disappointed since we had arrived on the scene too late to witness the flare-ups ourselves. Once again we could do little more than assure the family that no harm would come to them, but we also urged them to call us immediately if anything more happened in the future.

It wasn't long before our chance came. Mrs. Thomas placed an almost frantic call to Raymond only a few weeks later, reporting that her house had been the scene of considerable disturbances since 3:00 that afternoon. It all started while she was working at her drafting board. She told Raymond that several of her drafting tools kept moving by themselves. (She had lost no time placing most of them back in their tool box!) Telekinesis then broke out in the house and continued all day long. Even as she spoke to Raymond on the phone, she claimed that a drafting pencil was trying to raise itself from the drafting board. It was cavorting about right as they spoke!

I was unavailable that evening, but Raymond rushed over to the Thomas residence alone. He arrived fifteen minutes after receiving the frantic call. Mrs. Thomas was still visibly shaken and alone in the house, for she had sent her daughter out of the house to keep her from any harm. She was so frightened that (as Raymond told me later) her hands were shaking and she could hardly even pour a cup of coffee. She desperately wanted Raymond to believe her story and showed him her drafting table. He was able to examine several irregular scars that had apparently been made when Mrs. Thomas's tools began sliding over it telekinetically. Several of the tools were still on the floor where they had originally fallen.

It was Raymond's feeling that it might be possible to witness the PK effects for himself. In order to encourage another incident, he decided to leave the house after Mrs. Thomas finished her story. It is a well-known (though aggravating) principle that hauntings and poltergeists love to act up as soon as everybody turns their backs. So Raymond decided to play the game according to the poltergeist's own rules. He stepped out of the house for a few minutes at 8:00 P.M., leaving Mrs. Thomas still inside. She began picking up more of her tools as Raymond walked out the door, and proceeded to place them back in the tool box.

Raymond returned about seven minutes later, and he certainly saw a strange sight when he looked through the screen door. Mrs. Thomas was standing in the middle of the room almost in tears. Her tools (which were all very delicate and expensive) were strewn pell-mell over the living room floor. She immediately told Raymond that the box had overturned of its own accord just after his exit, and that the tools catapulted right out of it. Raymond didn't think Mrs. Thomas would deliberately damage her expensive equipment, so he decided to examine the scene in more detail. This is when he made a curious discovery. When he bent over to examine and help clear up the disarray, he found that the tools and the tool box were covered by some sort of moist residue. Now just how this residue came to be there represented quite a mystery, though this same phenomenon has been known to crop up in other cases. It was just one more feature of a genuinely puzzling case.

The episode of the catapulting drafting tools represented the finale to the case, however. From that day forward, no further strange events disturbed the peaceful home of Mrs. Thomas and her family. The psychic outbreaks seemed to end as suddenly and mysteriously as they had begun. This abrupt turn of events also alerted us to the fact that we were probably misdiagnosing the case. We had undertaken our investigation on the assumption that we were dealing with a bona fide haunting. This was obviously a mistake. For even though the phenomena the Thomases originally reported to us typically occurs in traditional "haunted houses," it now became clear that we were up against a poltergeist. The case had transformed right under our noses.

Unfortunately, we were never able to get to the root of the case. We eventually learned that Mrs. Thomas was rather dissatisfied with her work and her domestic life. But then, lots of people are. The fact that the outbreak was short, dynamic, and ceased suddenly nonetheless indicates that the *cause* of the problem probably related more to the people in the house than with the residence itself.

INVESTIGATING A FAMILY WITH A "HAUNTED" HISTORY

Hauntings and poltergeists are relatively rare events. Encountering one in a lifetime is unusual enough, but a few lucky (?) people just seem to keep running into them. When I first started investigating cases involving repeated hauntings of the same people, I was skeptical. It just sounded like too neat a pattern to be true. It wasn't for several years that I realized that perhaps some people are specifically prone to hauntings. These people seem gifted with the capacity to trigger hauntings wherever they go.

The case that alerted me to this possibility dates back to 1973, and it still represents one of my personal favorites. I learned of the case initially from Raymond, when he was called by the concerned family that August. The disturbances were focusing on a young couple, the Ceccatos, and their four-year-old daughter. The residence was an apartment building in Van Nuys, California. Their own apartment was not actually part of the main complex, but consisted of the manager's quarters attached to the rear of the small building. I was out of town when the case first started and only joined it after Raymond's field investigation was well in progress.

It turned out that Mr. Alfred Ceccato, age twenty-eight, and the manager of the building, was relatively unconcerned about the events disrupting his apartment. His call to the Southern California Society for Psychical Research (who referred him to us) was actually made at the urging of his wife. She was very frightened by the fearful poundings that would sometimes explode from the walls of the apartment, and the young couple told Raymond that they were even willing to take a polygraph test to prove the truth of their claims. It may seem odd that Mr. Ceccato was so unconcerned about this eruption of noise and minor telekinesis in his own home, but that was because he was so familiar with them. It turned out that he had apparently lived in several haunted houses over the years—and periodically just kept running into them. This claim alerted us to an intriguing possibility: perhaps Mr. Ceccato was somehow integrally linked to the production of these repeated disturbances. If we took those earlier episodes into account, the case we were now dealing with spanned well over thirteen years!

I learned about Mr. Ceccato and his psychic life when Raymond and I met with him in September at his apartment. He told me that he could recall hearing similar poundings and mysterious footsteps as a child in his parents' house located out of state. He had even written a short story based on his experiences when he was in high school. He most vividly recalled one incident that he shared with his brother. They were at home alone one afternoon, he told us, when they heard what sounded like someone walking across the roof. When they ran out and climbed up to see what was causing the noise, they saw the gravelly pebbles that covered the roof moving and sliding about. It looked like someone was shuffling through them. This rather surprised them since there was no wind blowing that afternoon, nor was there anyone actually on the roof.

When the family moved to Los Angeles, the "family" ghost moved right along with them. They heard similar sounds in several residences they shared.

The middle-class suburb of Van Nuys, California, became home for Mr. and Mrs. Ceccato shortly after they were married. During their first year's stay there in a rented house, several minor poltergeist episodes flared up. They occasionally saw pictures rotating on the walls, while odd knockings repeatedly rapped on the front door—even though no one was there.

So why were they contacting us, if all of this was such old hat to them? It seems that this current outbreak was getting out of hand. The knockings were becoming more common and violent, and by July of 1973 small objects in the house began mysteriously disappearing and reappearing. But the crucial event that led the Ceccatos to contact us occurred on July 25 while the family was at dinner. They were sitting at the dining room table enjoying their meal when a candle flung itself from its place on the mantlepiece—no one was near it at the time. "The candle holder was against the wall," Mr. Ceccato later wrote in an account of the incident, "when for no apparent reason and with no visible outside force, the candle holder flew off the mantle, flying three feet away from the wall onto the floor and breaking." The couple was stunned.

The telekenetic disturbances in the apartment began escalating after the candle incident. Mrs. Ceccato finally lost all composure when she saw a small coffee table suddenly levitate and then plop back to the floor while she was vacuuming. "When I saw the table with both eyes and facing it," she later testified, "it was nearly 2 ½ to 3 inches off the ground." She was so terrified that she begged her husband to get some help to make the poltergeist stop. Things got worse during the course of the next month when even more telekinesis broke out. That's when they finally called the Southern California Society for Psychical Research.

By far the most terrifying experiences the family reported were the violent raps—which of course happens to be one of the poltergeist's favorite tricks. What was so curious about these noises was that they sometimes didn't follow normal acoustical principles. While they often sounded just like normal physical poundings, the noises sometimes did not travel or "carry" the way sound normally does. During one of our visits with the family in September, Mrs. Ceccato explained this unusual aspect of the poundings to us in some depth. Her most memorable encounter with the raps was of just this type, and it came one afternoon when she was home alone with her daughter.

> I was in the bathroom combing my hair," she explained, "and [my daughter] kept calling me. She was standing at the threshold of the kitchen. She kept calling me to come; I was hurrying and was a little bit amazed at the time but I came in to answer her. She said, "Listen to noise," pointing into the kitchen. I was standing at the kitchen door on the outside and I couldn't hear a thing. I stepped into the kitchen and there was a horrible pounding that was shaking the lamp in the kitchen. Not the one on the dining room table but the one in the kitchen. And yet you step back into the hallway and nothing. Not one sound.

The fact that the poundings did not conform to normal acoustical principles is itself evidence that they were being paranormally produced. By experimenting in the apartment ourselves during our visit, Raymond and I discovered that it was impossible to produce any noise in the kitchen that would not be heard out in the adjoining hallway. The living room, kitchen, and hallway were all compactly spaced in the apartment and any sound produced in one area automatically traveled to the others. It struck us that, in this specific case, the raps were able to produce some sort of "sphere of influence" and could only be heard when someone stepped into the kitchen. It might also be noted that such odd acoustical quirks are not at all rare, commonly erupting in haunted and poltergeist-ridden residences. They can take a variety of forms. Sometimes the witnesses will hear furniture moving around in an empty room, only to find nothing displaced upon investigation. Or sometimes the poltergeist will produce noises like crockery being violently broken but without so much as damaging a single plate. So the "sounds" so often heard in these infested homes can be both "physical" and nonphysical at the same time. The Ceccatos were certainly not describing anything new or—for hauntings!—out of the ordinary.

We followed this case for several weeks before it came to a rather dramatic climax. We knew that Mr. Ceccato's strongest desire was to tape record the poundings, and his opportunity finally came on September 20. The young man was home alone at the time the pounding broke out, so we have only his own testimony to go by. But he called us as soon as he made the tape, and he literally pleaded with us to come over and hear it. We were naturally excited, so Raymond visited him the next day. Mr. Ceccato himself was still very excited. He never stopped repeating that, as God was his witness, he was telling the truth. Truth was indeed becoming stranger than fiction. So before proceeding any further, the following represents Mr. Ceccato's story about how he came to record the raps:

About 5:20 P.M. I was lying in the bathtub. I was practically sound asleep. I heard what sounded like a loud muffled voice over a loudspeaker. I could not understand the voice, if it was in fact a voice.

I leaped out of the tub, wrapped a towel around myself and ran into the living room. I looked in front of the house to see if there was any sign of a public announcement system or systems. There was no such sign. I went into the backyard to look for the same thing. I found nothing. I heard no children or cars in the area. The sound lasted only a couple of seconds.

I started back to the bathroom to dry off. As I started to walk through the hall I heard the familiar poundings on the walls and the rattling of the ceramic pictures on the wall. I stopped in the hall to listen. In ten seconds the pounding had stopped. I told myself I was going to record the sounds if it killed me.

It took about four minutes to get and set up my tape recorder. I put the recorder on the laundry hamper in the

guest bathroom. I put the mike on the floor, turned the
volume all the way up, and turned the recorder on. I went
to the door of my bedroom, stood at the threshold and
stared at the recorder across the hall waiting for something
to happen. Less than one minute later the pounding started.
It's now about 5:30 P.M. After the pounding on the wall, I
heard and recorded fourteen sounds that represented footsteps.

The tape itself lasts only about forty seconds. You can hear a
terrible din of quick rappings and rattlings, since the noise generated by the raps is being augmented by the reactive jigglings of
the ceramic pictures mounted on the wall from where, apparently, the raps were emanating. A few seconds of silence inter-
vene, and then come a series of fourteen incredibly loud blows.
These bangs sound as if someone were hitting the floor or a wall
with a sledge hammer. These "footsteps," as Mr. Ceccato desig-
nated them, occur every two seconds or so and come rhythmi-
cally. Echo-like dull thuds can be heard after each blow.

Our investigation of this case lasted over several weeks, and
we were eventually able to talk with a number of additional witnesses. These included a few of Mr. Ceccato's relatives who
kindly verified some of the incidents the young man reported
from his childhood. The combined and impressive testimony led
us to believe that Mr. Ceccato was telling us the truth about his
strange experiences and his "haunted" life. It therefore seemed
logical for us to conclude that this puzzling man was somehow
responsible for the troubles his family had confronted for so
many years. The manifestations he has been witnessing all his life
appear to be an outgrowth from some psychic talent lying within
him . . . but annoyingly out of his conscious reach.

I have gone into considerable depth about these three very different families and their "hauntings" to prove that nothing in the
psychic world is clean-cut and predictable. What appear on the
surface to be paranormal "visitations" by "entities" independent
of the family may in fact be disguised poltergeists. I do not mean
to suggest, however, that all haunted houses are created by the

people living in them. Some cases definitely represent the activity of some intelligence or force linked to the residence itself.* These strange places might be called "true" hauntings. Of course there also exists a discrete poltergeist syndrome, which was so well exemplified by the case presented in Chapter 2. But between these two separate dimensions of the psychic world lay several shades of grey, and these are the cases that are too often ignored by students of the paranormal. Both hauntings and poltergeists result from the activity of a localized and focalized psychic vortex, which may become activated under a variety of different circumstances.

Saying that the Roses, Mrs. Thomas, and Mr. Ceccato created the hauntings they were witnessing may be a bit unfair, though. This idea suggests that they possessed some sort of mysterious psychic power that they were projecting (albeit unconsciously) into their homes. This may be true, but there is another possibility with which we have to contend. Perhaps these people actively served as psychic *catalysts* to the events they witnessed. Perhaps they somehow possess the ability to activate strange but latent forces already existing in the houses where they live. If such were the case, we might say that a poltergeist haunting erupts when the psychic powers of the witness(es) interacts with a (usually) dormant force already present in the house . . . but beyond the perception and reach of most of us.

---

*For a case that I personally investigated and confronted, see Chapter 3 of my *The Haunted House Handbook* (New York: Tempo, 1978).

7

Diagnosing a Family Poltergeist

Tommy was on his scratched and bloody knees, crawling on all fours up the hallway. He was terrified and out of touch with reality. His only desire was to get out of his bedroom and get to his parents in the apartment's living room. Cries and screams escaped from the thirteen-year-old youth as he tried to flee whatever horror was in his room.

"The faces are screaming at me," he kept whimpering. "Blood is all over the walls."

It took his mother over four days to calm him down. Only then would he allow his parents to leave him alone in the apartment. He hadn't let his mother even go into the bathroom without tagging along. To all appearances the boy was going through some sort of psychotic episode, but his mother refused to dismiss the possibility that there was more to it than just that. For a poltergeist started menacing the apartment soon afterward.

This was certainly one of the most dramatic stories I'd ever heard during the course of my many ghost-hunts. It was also the precipitating event that somehow triggered a poltergeist haunting that lasted from November 1976 well into 1979 in the suburb of Woodland Hills, located outside central Los Angeles. The scene of the outbreak was a second-story, three-bedroom apartment set in an ugly stucco building consisting of several such units. Similar post–World War II apartment buildings comprised the entire street, which was located directly across from a poorly kept city park. My introduction to the case came in August of 1978, when Mrs. Harry Dell—one of the residents—phoned me to report her poltergeist problem. She was hoping I could get rid of the annoyances that were plaguing the apartment she shared with her husband and her teenaged daughter. This call was just the beginning of a rather lengthy investigation that would occupy me part-time from August until January of the next year.

I only later learned that Mrs. Dell's family also included two sons and another daughter, but none of these siblings were living at home during the active phases of my investigation. There was, however, at least one outside witness who was willing to talk to me about her experiences with the Dells' "haunted" apartment. This woman lived in the apartment directly below the Dells', but I only met her after my investigation was well in progress.

I visited the Dells' apartment three times between August 1978 and January 1979, but kept in phone contact with them regularly during this period. The events that were plaguing their rather drab complex were more episodic and unpredictable than most poltergeists tend to be, so I was never able to witness any of the outbreaks myself. Frankly, I never thought I would, because my first impression was that I was dealing with a true haunting. It was only later that I realized that a poltergeist was loose in their domicile . . . but it was an altogether different kind of poltergeist than I was used to studying.

When you seriously study parapsychology, you learn a basic set of principles about the poltergeist. These were the principles that I outlined in the previous chapter and to which the case recounted in Chapter 2 so classically conformed. You learn that poltergeists are generally short-lived outbreaks of violent psychokinesis that focus on a disturbed adolescent living in the besieged residence. The outbreak seems symbiotically linked to this "agent," who is usually repressing a great deal of hostility and aggression. The poltergeist is actually the very vehicle by which this aggression is being given unconscious expression. We all learn these principles, and only recently have they begun to be challenged. By and large, though, most poltergeist cases genuinely conform to them, so there is some value in learning these guidelines. But as I tried to show in the last chapter, it is sometimes difficult to differentiate poltergeists from hauntings, which is why I originally began wondering if the two might not be more closely linked than we've previously suspected. Some of the cases presented earlier in this book suggest just this: that it is not necessarily true that poltergeists express repressed hostility while hauntings do not. The same kind of psychodynamics may underlie both types of infestation in certain cases. The question we must still answer, however, is why the phenomena sometimes differ between poltergeists and what I like to call poltergeist hauntings.

The key to the answer lies in the fact that poltergeists tend to stem from individual personal problems while poltergeist hauntings sometimes stem from more subtle *family* problems. In some of the cases I've been able to investigate, it seems as though entire families were jointly projecting their poltergeists. For some reason these cases tend naturally to mimic true hauntings.

The case that first alerted me to this possibility was one I investigated in 1973. Since I've written this case up in detail in an earlier book, it will only be briefly described here.* The case concerned the complaints of a Mr. and Mrs. James Carter, who lived in a fashionable upper-middle-class home in the San Fernando Valley, a major suburb of Los Angeles. Their household included their five children, who were aged from eleven to seventeen. They had lived in their home for thirteen years before a brief flurry of poltergeist displays led one of their relatives to phone UCLA. The university suggested that I be called in on the case. The events plaguing the house were fairly typical for a true haunting. Beginning in November 1972, the family began hearing footsteps in the house, breathing sounds, and cold breezes mysteriously wafted down the hallway. These strange events soon began escalating. There were object-movements, a radio

---

*See my *The Poltergeist Experience* (New York: Penguin, 1979), pp. 275–82.

once changed stations by itself, closet clothes-hangers were found placed in bizarre positions, and a genuine apparition was seen one night. By the time the family phoned me, the events were focusing on the bathroom, where several incidents were being noted. I was not able to personally witness any of these events, but the family introduced me to several friends of theirs who were willing to corroborate the accounts.

What so struck me about this case was how the events began by mimicking a conventional haunting, complete with cold breezes, footsteps, and even a ghost. Only later did it accelerate into a somewhat active poltergeist. When I first spoke with the family on the phone, I even believed I was up against a good old-fashioned haunted house. My change of mind only came when I met them later that day and learned more about their problem.

While conversing with the family, I was able to discern that their home was the breeding ground for a great deal of unfocused frustration. The entire family wanted to move out of the house and back to South America, where they once had lived. Their plans were being repeatedly thwarted, and the outbreak seemed to be reflecting their frustration. It appeared to be a symbolic attack on the house they wanted so desperately to leave. It was clear that the Carters did not realize the link between the outbreak and their problem, but they freely vented their frustrations during a family "rap" session I organized with them during my second visit to their home. It soon became the focal point of this discussion. The results of the session were quite interesting, as well. The poltergeist activity ceased immediately! It was my feeling that the cure was probably affected by the family itself, as the members opened up and allowed themselves to verbally express their conflicts and frustrations. The upshot of this investigation also led me to believe that some poltergeists are reactions to family situations and do not necessarily focus on any one particular family member—that is, sometimes a family will act cooperatively to produce a poltergeist. I also began thinking, based on the paranormal dynamics of this case, that perhaps family-generated poltergeists will mask their true nature by mimicking a haunting.

The only problem with this line of thinking was that my theories about the Carter case were pretty subjective. I was never able to collect objective evidence that proved my view, and my only tools were my clinical impressions and instincts. Although it seemed obvious that the rap session had "exorcised" the poltergeist, the possibility that some other factor (even coincidence) led to the cessation of the psychokinesis could not be dismissed. My only recourse was to wait for a similar case to come my way, then use it to collect better evidence to support and document my views.

This was the possibility that presented itself five years later when the Dells contacted me. Through this case I was able to demonstrate that some poltergeists focus on whole families rather than on an individual member . . . and that these cases tend to be more subtle than your typical adolescent-triggered poltergeist.

Whatever force was loose in the Dells' apartment first broke forth in November 1976. The fateful evening began innocuously enough with a family game of Monopoly between Mr. and Mrs. Dell and three of their children. (These were by Mrs. Dell's first marriage.) Only their oldest boy, Tommy, wasn't participating, since he had secluded himself in his room earlier in the evening. Ten o'clock rolled around and it certainly looked as though the night was going to end as uneventfully as it had begun. By this time, Mrs. Dell was in the bathroom brushing her teeth before retiring, while the Dell children were busy packing up the game. That's when—to the family's utter horror—Tommy burst out of his room panic stricken and with a wild look on his face. His knees were carpet-burned and bloody, since he had apparently stumbled while trying to get out of his room. He was totally out of touch with reality and kept screaming that faces were shrieking at him from the windows of his room. His own mother's was one of them, and he saw blood oozing from the walls. He couldn't even walk, but crawled and stumbled up the hallway.

"My husband and I tried to take him back into his room," Mrs. Dell was to tell me two years later, "to show him there was nothing there after calming him down to a . . . vibrating shiver. There was nothing bleeding in there."

But in light of the many subsequent events she and her family shared in the apartment, she added that "just because I didn't see anything doesn't mean he didn't."

It took several days before Tommy's fright and anxiety ebbed and the family was able to return to normal. The Dells briefly explored hospital treatment for their son, but couldn't find any units willing to take an adolescent his age. Since the teenager seemed to come out of the psychosis by himself, they did not try to find out what caused the episode. It was only later that they realized that this strange event either catalyzed or heralded the arrival of the poltergeist in their apartment.

The cause of this "attack" was, in fact, never resolved. By the time I was brought in on the case, Tommy was no longer living at home and I couldn't discuss it directly with him. My personal suspicions were that the episode was probably not a true psychotic attack, but perhaps a drug reaction or a psychotic episode prompted by drug use. It was sad but true that the youth was a drug abuser, so this line of speculation strikes me as the most viable solution to that part of the mystery. (Even though true visual hallucinations are not produced by most psychedelic drugs, the content of Tommy's bizarre "trip" is consistent with the possibility that he had smoked some marijuana laced with phencyclidine, or "angel dust.") During the course of the current investigation, Tommy was undergoing drug rehabilitation treatment, which was the primary reason I was never able to talk with him.

It was only a few weeks later that Mrs. Dell began thinking that there was something unusual about the apartment. Mysterious footsteps sounded in the residence at night, and the frightened woman began feeling that some sort of "presence" was stalking the apartment. These sensations were rather vague, but they gradually became more distinct and represented the first phase of the psychic attack. When I first met Mr. and Mrs. Dell, both of them testified to the reality of the "presence." Their sixteen-year-old daughter Terri reported run-ins with the "ghost" as well.

It was apparently Mrs. Dell who first took note of the eerie visitor, while the family was still recuperating from the shock of their son's breakdown the month before. "It was just the feeling that something was staring at me," explained Mrs. Dell. "Just the feeling of a presence. I couldn't walk down the hallway without getting prickly feelings at my back. I felt the presence of something, and every time I walked down the hallway I felt I had to hurry up and get out of there.

"It was like a suffocating feeling, like something was going to enshroud me. Nothing ever did and nothing ever touched me. It was just an overwhelming feeling like something was going to. In my room it felt as though someone was looking at me. If my door wasn't shut or just ajar, I felt like something was going to burst right through it instantly."

The other members of the family readily corroborated Mrs. Dell's testimony.

I could tell from her voice that Mrs. Dell was no longer too fearful of the activity. It seemed that she had gotten used to it. But a ghost is a ghost, and the looks I saw in the faces of the other family members as she spoke belied a deeper concern with the problem. It was clear to me that Mr. Dell, too, was confused by the events plaguing the apartment, but he remained unusually quiet all during my visit. It struck me that he was simply detaching himself from the situation . . . from his family, from the haunting, perhaps even from his own fears. The whole atmosphere struck me as rather strange, almost as though there was a silent conspiracy underfoot that I didn't know about.

I actually found visiting the apartment that night very uncomfortable, although I tended to put my feelings down to the tension rife within the household.

Despite his detachment, Mr. Dell did not challenge his wife's testimony. He agreed with everything she was telling me. He even admitted that, before hearing of his wife's experiences, he too had similar feelings of the presence. He explained that he was napping in the afternoon one day when he woke with the feeling that someone was staring at him. He immediately rolled over to glare at the doorway of the bedroom, only to see that nobody was there. The episode made him feel so uneasy that he eventually got up and closed the door. It wasn't until some months later that he learned that his experiences dovetailed with those of his wife. He was obviously relieved to learn of his wife's encounters, and he told me that he was glad to know that he wasn't simply imagining things.

It appeared that most of the Dell children were too young to realize what was going on in the apartment. They didn't seem bothered by the presence, and Tommy (no longer concerned with his previous bizarre episode) certainly never mentioned anything about it to his parents. It is possible, however, that he was afraid of what they might think should he start up again with any "crazy" talk. But the paranormal activity, far from going away, soon began to escalate. Mysterious noises and more footsteps started plaguing the apartment next.

"I often heard footsteps in the hallway," Mrs. Dell told me during both my first and second visits. By no means was that all she heard.

"One night," she explained to me, "I heard what sounded from my place in the bedroom, like someone was pulling out drawers in the kitchen and rustling with the silverware. On another time late at night I heard what sounded like chairs being picked up and thrown over the floor." She invariably investigated the house, but never found anything in the kitchen actually disturbed.

By this time it was December and the "ghost" decided it was time to get more physical. "I was going down the hallway," explained Mrs. Dell about one of her subsequent experiences, "and as I turned on the light and got ready to move further down the hall, it went off. I assumed that it had been switched off by the sleeve of my robe; it's a pretty full sleeve. It was two weeks later that I walked through the hall, turned on the light in the hall, got all the way down to my bedroom door, and it turned off by itself."

These curious sounds and manifestations served only to augment the feeling of the "presence." The presence came and went during December and the following January. It sometimes could be felt strongly in the residence, while on other occasions it would become nearly indistinct.

The history of the poltergeist haunting becomes a little confusing at this point, since there were several changes within the family that kept them from keeping track of the disturbances.

It was during the next few months that Terri decided to leave home and live with her fiancée, while Tommy's problems were becoming so unmanageable that he was sent to a youth camp. Despite these changes in the composition of the family, the Dells decided to stay in their apartment along with their three remaining younger children. Even though the family was undergoing its fair share of readjustments, Mrs. Dell assured me that the haunting was as active as ever between January and June 1977. She explained that the footsteps, sounds, and even some additional minor poltergeist actions kept breaking out then and over the next six months. Even the younger children finally seemed to pick up on the presence and complained of sensing it. Mrs. Dell took a commonsense attitude toward her children's claims and did not encourage them to talk about it. Her first impression was that perhaps they were imagining it all, since it was possible that the younger children were merely reacting to conversations they might have overheard between her husband and herself. Talk of the invisible presence was becoming common between them through the weary months of early 1977.

Things started picking up with renewed forcefulness in June 1977 when Terri returned home with her baby. Things hadn't worked out too well with her boyfriend, so she thought her best bet was simply to return home. Everyone in the family was quite sure of what happened next.

Terri corroborated her mother's accounts for me by adding her own testimony about the events that accompanied her return home. She had her own ghostly encounter only two days after she returned. "It was night," she told me. "While I was laying in bed and my Mom was asleep and the lights were off, I thought I heard my Dad coming down through the hall. I sat up in bed and then looked around the corner and there was nobody there."

That wasn't the end of the eerie encounter either: "But the noise of the walking in the hallway continued," Terri went on to say. "It sounded like someone was pacing because they were nervous or something—just back and forth, back and forth. Then it stopped." Terri concluded her story by adding that she witnessed several of these exhibitions over the next several weeks. The noise of chairs and silverware being rattled in the kitchen continued throughout the summer as well, sometimes even waking the Dells in the middle of the night.

Despite all the ghostly activity, many months passed before the Dells came to the reluctant conclusion that they needed help. So far the haunting, or whatever it was, really wasn't bothering them too much. They realized it was all weird enough, but it seemed so harmless and the family eventually even got used to it. They jokingly started calling their unwanted visitor "Casper" after the friendly ghost of cartoon fame. The younger children settled down, too, and Mrs. Dell began to think that they simply weren't being bothered by the strange sounds rampant in the residence. The manifestations died down by the end of 1977, and the Dells began thinking that perhaps their ghost had finally left.

But they were wrong! When the next summer came, a flurry of events so agitated Mrs. Dell that she finally contacted me after learning about my interest in ghosts, hauntings, and poltergeists. There were actually two precipitating incidents (in August) that led the distraught woman to call me, the first coming while she was taking a shower.

"I was in the shower in the middle of the afternoon," she told me when I first investigated the case. "It seemed like the sun was coming in and out of the clouds. It was real fast like how you see in the *Time Machine*. [Mrs. Dell was apparently describing her perceptions from within the shower stall. The lighting in the room looked as though it was strobing, which was the effect used in the celebrated movie version of H. G. Wells's *The Time Machine*. In that film, rapid sunsets and sunrises strobe at an incredible rate to denote the passage of eons.] I wiped my eyes, but it was still occurring. I thought that something was in my eyes and making the lighting appear that way."

When the puzzled woman finally opened the shower door, she was in for quite a surprise.

"I happened to look at the mirror . . . at the light above the mirror," she said, "and it was going on and off. I peeked a little bit further and I saw my light switch going on and off."

This claim was so intriguing that I questioned Mrs. Dell closely about the matter. She never wavered in her assertion that she actually saw the switch turning itself on and off repeatedly and quickly.

It was unfortunate that there was no other witness to this uncanny incident. Terri was the only other family member at home that afternoon, but she was in the living room and didn't notice the flickerings. But she had her own ghostly encounter later that night. This was the second crucial event leading to my entry into the case.

This incident actually occurred the next morning at about 5:00 A.M. Terri explained that her baby was just waking up, and she was getting up to give him a feeding. She was walking across the hallway to the bathroom when she saw a large bulky shadow coming toward her from the other direction. Her first impression was that her father was up and about, but she soon realized that the figure wasn't physical at all and comprised *just* a shadow. The teenager was so frightened that she rushed to the bathroom, but no sooner was she safely there than a large picture on the hallway wall began swinging by itself. Not only did it swing back and forth, but it actually banged up against the wall. It caused quite a racket.

These forceful physical manifestations now breaking out in the apartment succeeded where the footsteps, breathings, and nightly noises had failed. They totally demoralized the family—and that's when they called on me to see if I could help.

My own investigation of the case began at this point and lasted, as I indicated earlier, until the beginning of 1979. Since the active poltergeist phenomena was very sporadic and (frankly) not all that eventful, I didn't think I would be lucky enough to witness any of the psychokinesis myself. So most of my visits to the apartment involved taking down the family's testimony, talking with any outside witnesses I could find, and trying to discover the likely cause of the disturbances. There were few problems complicating my first goal, since the Dells were all eager to talk with me. I was also able to meet and talk with at least one outside witness of the Dells' poltergeist. This added testimony contributed appreciably to my feeling that the Dells were telling me the truth. During my second visit with the family, Mrs. Dell informed me that her downstairs neighbor (who lived directly under her own apartment) could corroborate the existence of the haunting. Needless to say, I didn't lose any time scurrying down to see if the lady was home. She was, and willingly provided me with her own statement about the Dells' problem.

This witness explained that she had been disturbed on several occasions by odd noises emanating from the Dells' residence. The noises were usually heard late at night. She would hear what sounded like people walking or running about, and sometimes she had to listen to the toilet flushing over and over again in rapid succession. Her first thought was that someone was sick, but when she checked with the Dells she discovered that the footsteps and other noises were sometimes occurring when everyone was asleep upstairs . . . or even when nobody was home!

Finding an explanation for the infestation took longer to discover. Since the Dells were eager for me to find the cause of the occurrences, I was obliged to meet their expectation. I must admit that I, too, was eager to find out what was causing the disturbances. Soon, though, I found myself focusing more on the psychological underpinnings of the case than on the events themselves. Even during my first visit to the house I could tell that there was a lot of anger present, especially between Mr. and Mrs. Dell. The family was undergoing a great deal of pressure because of their purely parapsychological problems, however, so I tended to discount the possibility that psychological dynamics were complicating the case. *Every* family has its fair share of problems, frustrations, and petty annoyances to deal with, and certainly the Dells didn't strike me as worse off than many other families I've visited socially. Given the circumstances under which they were living, I thought they were doing rather well.

My very first impression was that the case represented a true haunting more than a typical poltergeist. Remember that the primary phenomena reported by the family consisted of a presence in the apartment, eerie footsteps, and the "ghost" Terri saw one morning. Such phenomena are more typical of a haunting than a poltergeist, but this wasn't the only characteristic of the case that kept me from initially diagnosing the case correctly. The long and rather intermittent duration of the outbreaks was also atypical of the classic poltergeist, nor did the events seem to be focusing on any special person in the household. The two most likely agents for the poltergeist theory were Tommy and Terri; but the Dells convinced me that the outbreaks had continued even during their children's prolonged absences from the apartment. But neither could the case be considered totally impersonal. The outbreaks—while not focusing on any particular member of the family—*did* seem to relate to stresses within it. It was very suspicious that the events were temporally linked to Tommy's frightening "psychotic" episode. While the activity in the apartment remained intermittent over the next two years, it tended to reactivate most aggressively whenever Terri returned home after long periods of absence. (Between 1976 and 1978, she had lived away from home twice.) I was also intrigued when Mrs. Dell told me how, some years earlier, she had witnessed a similar poltergeist attack in another apartment in Los Angeles. She had lived there with her children before her second marriage, and the events so frightened her that she moved out of the building the very night of the outbreak.

These conflicting patterns led me to believe that I was dealing with a family-generated poltergeist that was only masquerading as a so-called haunting. I did not want to base this diagnosis solely on clinical observations, however—the mistake I had already made once while studying the Carter case in 1972. I realized that I now had the chance to put my theories to the test, and I didn't want to lose it.

But just how could I proceed? The best path I could think of was to conduct psychological testing on all the family members crucial to the outbreak—Mrs. Dell, her husband, and Terri. I came to this conclusion in September 1978 after working with the family for two months. By that time I knew the family trusted me, and I was delighted when they all agreed to take part in the assessments. The only problem I faced was choosing which tests to use, and to figure out a way to implement the examination so that I could objectively evaluate the results. Since my plan was to use "projective" tests, which can be rather freely interpreted by the psychologist examining them, I didn't want to analyze them myself. I was simply too close to the case to make a fair appraisal of what the tests were showing. Luckily, it didn't take me long to determine a method I could use to evaluate the Dell case. My plan required the services of one of my professional colleagues, so my investigation soon became a joint effort—with me working from Los Angeles and a colleague/psychologist working from New York.

My course of action went into effect in October. I began by positing a theory about what I expected or hoped to find in the test results. My prediction was that each of the Dells would show the *personality patterns and characteristics we normally associate with the typical poltergeist agent.* I therefore expected that all of the Dells suffered from pent-up and poorly expressed aggressions and hostility, and that these patterns would show up in the results. Such a finding would suggest that their aggressions were being expressed in the outbreaks so disturbing to them.

Of course, I didn't tell the family what I was expecting to find. When I met with them later that month to implement the testing, I told them only that I was curious about the dynamics of their family life. They were assured that the results of the test would help me learn a little more about them as people. With these factors in mind, the Dells cooperated in completing three sets of tests for me. These consisted of three rather standard psychological tests widely used by clinicians in this country:

1. I began by having them take a version of the *House-Tree-Person* test, in which each of the Dells drew their version of a house, a tree, and both a male and female figure.

2. The second test I administered was the *Rosenzweig Picture-Frustration Study.* This test had never been used before during the assessment of a poltergeist case. It consists of a series of cartoons that present potentially frustrating situations. Captions are totally omitted from the pictures, and the client or respondent is asked to fill them in.

3. My final test was the famous *Rotter's Incomplete Sentence Blank,* which —as its name suggests—consists of several sentences that the client or respondent completes.

Now just why had I chosen these particular tests?

My choice was based on my need to find a few easily

executed tests that would enable me, or a psychologist evaluating them, to judge several different personality characteristics of the Dells and their home life. The first test (as described above) helps to understand how a person views himself or herself and adapts to the social environment, while the second is excellent for discovering the strategies the respondent uses when dealing with frustration and anger. The last test I used can help the clinician study the respondent's fantasy life and the "gestalt" of his or her self-view and of life in general. Both the first and third tests are good for studying the defenses put up in the course of the client's social life. My feeling was that any good clinician evaluating all these test results could supply me with a pretty good (and objective) view of the Dells—both by way of their individual psychologies and their family dynamics. These tests are also rather fun to take, so the Dells were able to get their minds off their "ghost" for a while during their execution.

The day after my session with the Dell family, by prior agreement I sent the responses to Dr. Gertrude Schmeidler, a psychologist at the City College in New York. Dr. Schmeidler is also a seasoned parapsychologist and was more than willing to cooperate in the study. To insure that she gave me as unbiased an evaluation as possible, I told her nothing about the Dells other than that they were being plagued by a poltergeist. Since it was reasonable to assume that her bias would be to identify a single poltergeist agent on the basis of the tests, I explained in my cover letter that these test results did *not* include those of the likely agent. (This wasn't really dishonest since I didn't believe there *was* just one agent in this case.) I certainly didn't let Dr. Schmeidler know that I expected *each* of the family members to be harboring frustrations and repressed hostilities, nor did I give her any clues about the theory I was testing out. But to my delight, she found just what I was expecting.

Even though Dr. Schmeidler was very busy, she was able to get back to me by the end of the month. She eventually wrote up two reports for me. The first consisted of a detailed examination of each of the people involved in the disturbances, while the second was a shortened summary of the first set of evaluations.

The first thing Dr. Schmeidler pointed out to me (through our subsequent correspondence) was that all three family members were indeed trying to deal with a high degree of aggression in their interpersonal relationships. She explained how surprised she was to find an astonishingly large number of similar themes cropping up in their test results. "Outstanding in each of them," she told me, "is aggression directed against others—as opposed to the self-punishing of the mute, minimized kind." This is exactly what I expected to find, for it indicated that each of the Dells tended to lash out in the face of frustration by blaming others for his/her problems. The Dells did not seem to internalize the hostility by blaming themselves, or by attempting to ignore it.

But the key to my hypothesis was that the Dells habitually relied on repression to keep from acting on their aggressions. And by studying Dr. Schmeidler's report, this pattern was clearly evident. It was least applicable to Terri, even though she revealed herself as a young woman incapable of handling even minor frustrations or of entering into helping relationships with the rest of her family. But the use of repression to handle life stresses was very evident in the test results procured from both Mr. and Mrs. Dell. For example, Dr. Schmeidler's report on Mrs. Dell emphasized that she was vainly trying to repress her own marital and personal problems. The key words in her psychological profile were," . . . she's closed up the vent to her problems; she tries not to let any of it come out."

This is exactly the pattern you find when examining poltergeist agents, so this case was running true to form.

I was particularly interested in what Mr. Dell's results would show, since he was such an enigma to me. He always appeared stoic and detached, and during the course of my investigation I wondered if this detachment was some sort of defense he used to deal with his family and his life. My impressions were partially borne out by the profile I received from my colleague, who found Mr. Dell to be coping with an extraordinarily high aggression level, mostly stemming from feelings of personal insecurity. His test results indicated that he, too, was the sort of person who tends to blame others for his own problems, but who relies on psychological repression to deal with his feelings of anxiety and inadequacy. In fact, his test results indicated a potential for physical violence. These were being kept in check, thankfully, by his strong defenses.

It was somewhat surprising to learn that Terri's relationship with her parents was generally healthy, but that the Dells' marital adjustment was extremely poor.

I suppose the best evaluation of the case came by way of some remarks Dr. Schmeidler made in a letter to me later that month. "These are fascinating, wild, bizarre records from the poltergeist . . . family," she wrote. "If you hadn't told me that none of them was from the agent, I would have been in trouble —because each of them is so aggressive and strange that I'd have thought any of them was *it.*"

By the conclusion of my investigation of the Dell case, I believed that the poltergeist was generated by their own unhappiness. I saw no reason to suggest that an outside intelligence was invading their apartment. It was not a true haunting at all.

Though outwardly displaying the facade of a happy home, it became quite clear to me over the months that the Dells were a deeply troubled family. Not only had this pattern become clear to me as my work with them progressed, it also showed up rather clearly in their test results. Since I had a responsibility to help the family in any way I could, I knew that I would eventually have to share these findings and interpretations with them. That time came when Mrs. Dell called me only a few weeks after I had received the final evaluation from New York. She was calling to report that the poltergeist was acting up again, this time engaging in some rather impressive object-throwings. I knew I would now have to explain to her what I felt the source of her problem really was. I was a little apprehensive, since I really didn't know how she would take my advice: that family and marital counseling would help her more than an investigation or an exorcism.

Fate has a curious way of intervening during touchy moments such as this. Before I had a chance to counsel the Dells, Mrs. Dell told me that she and her husband were separating. The poltergeist had erupted, I then discovered, during the critical days when they were coming to this decision.

I can't say that I was surprised, and I couldn't help but wonder how the separation would affect the dynamics of the poltergeist. I later learned that the outbreaks permanently ceased after the breakup.

8

An "Out-of-Body" Poltergeist Strikes Home

The date was August 30, 1977. I had just arrived home from a trip to New York and was sitting at my desk contemplating three weeks of mail. I was a bit annoyed since I had expected to find my car waiting in the driveway. (I had left it with a friend who was caretaking my house in my absence.) But a moment later my car did come driving up. The front door burst open and an ex-tenant of mine walked directly into my study.

"Have you spoken to Dave yet?" he asked. He was alluding to his brother, whom I had left in charge of the house three weeks earlier.

"No," I replied.

"Some mighty strange things have been going on here while you've been away," he said with a sense of excitement in his voice.

Mike didn't have to say anything more, since I could tell exactly what he was talking about. So I merely told him that I would speak to Dave later on when he came back to the house. That his brother had experienced some "strange things" in the house while I was away didn't surprise me very much, for during my trip I had found myself "haunting" it from a distance! I knew that I had been successful even before I got home that warm August night.

In the past, parapsychologists have usually attributed the activity rife in so-called "haunted houses" to the ghostly doings of the dead. In this respect, probably the last word on the subject was contained in an analysis made in 1919 by Ernesto Bozzano in his classic book, *Les Phénomènes des hantise.* Bozzano was a brilliant scholar and an authority on hauntings. Not only did he note in his book that murders and other types of tragic deaths commonly take place in houses that later become haunted, he sought to *prove* the point. He had little difficulty showing that the apparitions seen in these unusual locations generally resemble people who once lived there and were the victims of these tragedies. He eventually analyzed 374 incidents of localized hauntings that he collected from several countries. Traditional "ghosts" were seen in 311 of these cases, and Bozzano was able to demonstrate that 117 of these ghosts resembled the former tenants of the houses in question. The ghosts were not immediately recognized by the witnesses in 41 instances, but were later found to be similar to figures depicted in old portraits or photographs of former residents.

Bozzano made another discovery during his research that wasn't as predictable. He pointed out in his encyclopedic study that some so-called ghosts seem to represent the apparitions of living agents! In other words, *some hauntings turn out to be produced by people who are still living!* He therefore concluded that not *all* hauntings are caused either by wandering spirits or by some sort of energy left behind by a person who had died tragically or suddenly.

Few researchers or writers on the subject today have said much about these "hauntings by the living," nor have they even bothered to concern themselves with this fascinating phenomenon. But the understanding of these strange cases is crucial to our understanding of the poltergeist. For it could be that hauntings and poltergeists are more closely connected than we have previously considered them to be. Perhaps some conventional "haunted houses," like the notoriously rambunctious poltergeist, are also caused by the psychic powers unleashed by the unconscious mind. Perhaps the witness to a haunting is more dynamically linked to the outbreak than he or she thinks. There is also considerable folklore suggesting that a particularly psychic person can "send" a poltergeist to an enemy, probably by sending a demon or an animal familiar to plague him. Some recent evidence could indicate that such a phenomenon actually exists—but that it has little to do with the satanic.

This was, in fact, just the sort of case I found myself grappling with in 1977. The case was especially provocative since it was *my* house that was suddenly becoming the scene of the poltergeist, and *I* was the purported ghost.

From the early months of 1974 until the end of 1978 I lived in a typical post–World War II tract home in Reseda, a suburb of Los Angeles right in the middle of the San Fernando Valley. I certainly had not chosen to buy the house because of any psychic intuition or any ghostly associations attached to it. The house went against every stereotype of your Hollywood-depicted haunted house: it was built in 1953 and no history of violence or tragedy was associated with it. Nor to the best of my knowledge had any of the previous tenants complained of paranormal disturbances there. It had been owned by the mother of a friend of mine, and I had originally leased it when the woman decided to move closer to the sunny beaches of California. When my landlady decided that it was time to unload the property, it was simply convenient for me to buy it. The house consisted of a living room, dining room, and three bedrooms that all entered onto a central hallway. The entrance to the hallway could be seen from the living room.

The story of the haunting/poltergeist begins on August 8, 1977, when I had to fly to New York on business. This was just one of many trips to New York I was making in those days and, since I planned to be away for three weeks, I asked a friend of mine to take care of the property in my absence. David Ostovich was a twenty-year-old printer, and I knew him well since his brother (Mike) was an erstwhile tenant of mine. This was not the first time that Dave had taken care of my house, since he enjoyed getting away from living with his family. He had little interest in the paranormal, though the subject would come up now and then in our conversations. Dave moved into my house on August 8 and stayed until August 30 when I arrived back home. Since he works during the day, he only stayed in the house in the evenings and at night.

During these same weeks, I was nestled snugly in an apartment in Long Island City, a community of mixed ethnic groups conveniently located only a few subway stops from downtown Manhattan. I really had no cause to contact Dave while I was gone, so I never spoke to him over the phone nor received any communications from him. I only learned that a poltergeist had been kicking up a fuss when I returned home.

But as I said earlier, I really knew about the infestation all along since, in a sense, I had been "sending" the poltergeist to him. My attempts at "haunting" my own house resulted when I found myself having vivid out-of-body experiences while in New York. Out-of-body experiences are strange episodes in which the experiencer feels as if his mind is functioning independently from the body. The study of the out-of-body experience is a subject very close to my heart because several years ago I had been engaged in a great deal of laboratory research in this area. I personally have also been having out-of-body experiences for years: I underwent a series of them when I was a very young child, and cultivated the knack of inducing them when I was a teenager. I must admit that it was a little disappointing to lose the ability as I grew older, but even to this day I undergo them sporadically. Nonetheless, I suddenly found myself undergoing a series of these journeys away from the body while in New York that summer, which allowed me to play a psychic joke on Dave back in Los Angeles . . . to his utter fright and eventual dismay!

I arrived in New York about midnight on the evening of Monday, August 8, and settled into my accommodations. Everything was going along just fine until I began experiencing odd "sinking" sensations before falling asleep during the following week. These experiences were very vivid, and on occasion I would find myself becoming totally paralyzed. They often lasted for several seconds. I wasn't frightened by these episodes, however, for in the past I have always associated them with the onset of my out-of-body experiences (OBEs). So I merely assumed that I was about to have another series of them.

I did not start having discrete OBEs, however, until my second week in New York. (This would roughly be August 15–22.) That's when I started having vivid "dreams" about returning to my home in Los Angeles that turned out to be more than *just* dreams.

These curious dream-OBEs, as I labeled them, were at first only vague and confusing, and I could remember relatively little about them when I awoke in the morning. But eventually they became more distinct. During each experience I would find myself in the hallway of my home, and would then walk either up or down the hallway looking or entering into each bedroom in turn. I always worry about my house when I am gone, so I guess I was merely using my out-of-body excursions to check on things.

As I just said, these experiences were at first rather nebulous. But within a few days I started waking up with the strong *inner* feeling that I had been out-of-body and back in Los Angeles. This sense of conviction was unmistakable. Since I have had years of experience with OBEs, I can easily recognize this feeling, which normally accompanies these strange journeys of the mind. But the experience that finally convinced me that I was going out-of-body came on the night of August 19.

That evening, after retiring and falling asleep, I found myself back in my Los Angeles home as usual. I did not experience actually leaving the body, which is a dramatic sensation that often accompanies the experience, but found myself occupying a lifelike apparitional representation of myself. It was easy for me to tell that I was out-of-body and not merely dreaming, since the two experiences are too subjectively different to be confused. I looked around, spotted my telephone (resting on a little table at the end of the hall), and walked down to it. Then I tried to do something rather absurd. I immediately thought about making a call to my colleague, Raymond Bayless, but I found that my fingers couldn't move the dial. I became rather frustrated.

"Wait a minute," I thought to myself. "I'm really in New York. I can't phone Raymond." After considering my situation for a moment, I decided it would be best for me to get back to my body. So I focused back on New York and blacked out.

I did not wake up after this experience and only arose several hours later. But when I did get up, I found myself retaining a perfect memory of the experience. Since I have had only one or two lucid dreams in my life, I naturally concluded that I had been projecting to my home in my sleep.*

In one sense I found this all rather surprising, since my last rash of frequent OBEs only occurred when I was a teenager, some ten years before. My out-of-body experiences had been more and more sporadic since that time. But the impression that I was now undergoing chronic OBEs was so strong that I felt I should tell someone about them. It was fortuitous that I was scheduled to visit a parapsychology laboratory in Brooklyn that afternoon, where an old friend of mine was then working as a researcher. Keith Harary is an exceptional psychic with whom I worked in 1973, and he is himself a gifted out-of-body traveler.† So that afternoon I filled him in on my experiences when we met at the division of parapsychology at the Maimonides Medical Center. His response was to encourage me to continue exploring them, and this advice spurred me on and made me resolve to really *work* with my experiences should they continue. Keith is sometimes capable of making the people whom he visits while out-of-body see him or respond to his presence, so I resolved to explore this possibility myself.

I had my next vivid OBE on the evening of August 22, just as I was expecting. This time, however, I tended to dismiss the experience as a dream since I did not realize how evidential it would ultimately turn out to be. Something happened during this episode that really threw me for a loop, and continued to puzzle me until I returned to Los Angeles.

I once again found myself walking up the hallway of the house during that night's astral excursion. I was determined to make my presence known to Dave this time, and the intention was foremost in my mind. I decided the best thing to do was to begin

---

*A lucid dream is a dream in which the experiencer realizes that he or she is dreaming.

†See my chapter "Experiments with Blue Harary" in my anthology *Mind Beyond the Body* (New York: Penguin, 1978).

by searching the house for Dave. My first goal was to go into the house's spare bedroom and see what I would find. I seemed to float into the room, and there I saw a sleeping figure in bed. Since my vision is often blurred while I'm experiencing an OBE, I had to look closely to see who it was. I was rather surprised when I realized that it wasn't Dave at all, but his brother Mike! The figure stirred as I was watching it, which startled me a bit and I left the room. My OBE came to an end only moments later.

I was very puzzled when I awoke back in New York. My experience certainly felt like a genuine OBE but, I wondered, why the hell was Mike sleeping in the house? There was simply no reason for him to be there. My first thought was that I had actually been misperceiving Dave, but even this rationalization didn't seem likely. Dave would have been sleeping in the master bedroom and not in the rather sparsely furnished spare room, I figured.

My (erroneous) assumption that my experience had actually been a dream of some sort seemed logical, though, since Mike was a former tenant. For six months in 1975–1976 he lived in the house and had occupied the very room in which I had "seen" him.

Gradually though, I began changing my opinion. The more I thought about this curious episode the more dissatisfied I became with the dream theory. It dawned on me that if I had been dreaming about Mike, I would have seen the spare room arranged the way Mike had decorated it when he was living there. But it wasn't. I saw it arranged just the way I left it before flying to New York. So eventually I came to the conclusion that I actually had experienced an OBE, but remained puzzled about Mike's presence in the house. Maybe it was Dave after all, I concluded. So I made a mental note to check with Dave when I returned home to see if he had "detected" my presence in any way.

This turned out to be my last OBE. I had no more after August 22, and the experiences and the sinking sensations all ceased abruptly. The stage was now set for my return home.

I first learned that my house had been the scene of some minor poltergeist phenomena from Mike the very evening of my return. He volunteered this information without any prompting on my part. Because I didn't want to influence Dave's testimony in any way or ask him any leading questions, I did not ask Mike to fill me in on the details. Instead I waited calmly for Dave to return, which he did late that night, and I learned of the events directly from him only a couple of hours later.

Dave was very excited when he got to the house about 10:00 P.M. and he seemed just bursting to tell me about his psychic adventures. What resulted was truly one of the most bizarre stories I've ever encountered as a ghost hunter, and far more engaging than my experiences in New York were leading me to suspect. Dave explained that strange noises had started manifesting in the house the very day that I left for New York. He at first didn't attribute them to anything paranormal. He merely thought that they were illusions created by the noise of the air conditioning unit that, owing to a heat wave that was hitting the city that month, he usually kept running when he was in the house.

"I got home from work probably eight o'clock that evening," he explained about his first day alone in the house, "and again we were experiencing really hot weather. So the first thing I did was flip on the air conditioning when I walked in. I noticed a couple of times small noises—rappings and what not—that I attributed to either the air conditioner, or the television or the stereo."

Dave went on to explain that he had heard these sounds almost nightly during the weeks of August 8 and August 15. But after the first few days, he began hearing what he could only describe as "moaning sounds." He actually described them as "low moanings" and said that they sounded as though they were made by a low "baritone voice." These experiences usually began about 6:30 P.M. Although puzzled by the sounds, Dave still did not realize that they were possibly paranormal until the evening of August 22. That's when an entire series of poltergeist phenomena broke out, culminating in the brief appearance of an apparition.

"That Monday was a pretty easy day [at work]," he explained. "So I was well rested and wasn't fatigued. I went from work to my parents' house to talk to my father, and stayed there until just a few minutes before 8:00 [P.M.]. Then I left my family's house to come here in order to change clothes and freshen up a bit."

Dave became a little nervous as he went on with his story:

> I don't think I got here any later than 8:05. So I was just going to freshen up, put on some different clothes, and go back to work. As a result, I knew I wasn't going to be here long, so I didn't bother turning on the air conditioner, didn't turn on the stereo, or anything. I was here approximately fifteen minutes and was sitting in the [master] bedroom putting on my shoes . . . when I heard a knocking at the front door. This was pretty close from where I was sitting as far as loudness.

For some reason it just "flashed" in Dave's mind that there really wasn't anyone at the door. He later told me that this feeling was a kind of uncanny "intuition," a sense that there was something odd about the knocking.

> Instead of getting up and answering it, my first instinct was that nobody was at the door. Before I could even begin to start to think about why I felt that way, I heard it again distinctly enough and loudly enough to rattle the brass door-knocker that's on the door . . .

> So that time I just got up and walked to the front door and opened it. There was nobody at the door and the screen [door] was latched. It wasn't locked. It was latched shut, it wasn't open, and I didn't hear anybody latching it as I was walking. So I looked toward both sides as I walked to the edge of the porch and walked around and there was nobody in view.

> About then I decided that something odd was definitely going on. And I walked back into the house, into the master bedroom again to put on my other shoe. This was just a matter of a few seconds. But then things started really moving fast with my mind. I mean to the extent that I wanted to finish up as quickly as possible and get out. It was then —I hadn't even finished putting on my shoe—when I heard the low moaning that I'd heard on several other occasions.

Dave subsequently told me that he could not ascertain from exactly where in the house the moaning emanated. He did say, though, that it was definitely from within the house and that it was produced by a deep masculine voice. He actually heard two moans, one after the other:

> I heard the first one and really started to panic. I was having trouble getting the shoe tied because I was shaking and trying to do it really quickly. And then I heard a really long moan.

> I never walked across your carpeting [in the living room] in my shoes because of the chance that ink was on them. So just by instinct, I went through the hall and through the kitchen. I was as close to running as you can get. I went out the front door, but didn't close it hard enough to latch it. At that time, I opened it approximately a foot and a half to two feet in order to slam it closed. At that time, something—you know, a figure—went by the [hallway] doorway. It was just "something" going by the doorway. It's very hard to have to describe . . . it's just the way it would look if you caught somebody who was almost out of view walking by a doorway. After that I slammed the door and it latched.

Dave interrupted his story by going into the hallway and showing me exactly what he had seen. The apparition seemed to be moving quickly by the doorway, walking to the south part of the house. Dave had not been able to see it clearly enough to determine if it were a male or female figure, whether it were clothed, or anything else that would have helped him identify it. However, while Dave was explaining all this, my mind wandered back to my friend Keith in New York, and it dawned on me that the apparition Dave was describing was similar to the type often reported by people who have been able to spontaneously detect OBE visitors. During the summer of 1973, I spent six weeks running experiments at the Psychical Research Foundation in Durham, North Carolina, with Keith. We wanted to see if, while out-of-body, he could travel to a distant lab room and make animals or people react to his presence. These experiments were very successful. We learned, for instance, that many volunteer subjects and even the experimenters conducting the tests would sometimes have spontaneous impressions or peculiar "feelings" at the very time that Keith was visiting the target area while out-of-body. Sometimes these detections were visual, and the subjects would briefly see odd light flashes or shadows, usually only out of the corners of their eyes. This seems to be the same sort of detection Dave underwent when he saw the apparition.

This was Dave's first encounter with the world of psychic phenomena, and it had a profound psychological effect on him. He was so frightened when he left the house that he jumped into his truck and drove away! However, he was only a few yards down the street when what he described to me on several occasions as an "uncanny sereneness" overcame him. All memory of the evening's experiences suddenly became blocked from his mind at that moment, and he suffered from a temporary and selective amnesia during which he remembered nothing about the moans, raps, and apparition he had witnessed only a few minutes earlier. (This odd reaction was most likely a form of amnesia brought about by the sort of trauma often experienced by accident victims.) Dave explained that he only recalled these traumatic events later that night when his brother came to visit him at work. Mike happened to mention my name, and this triggered the sudden and total return of his brother's memories about his experiences. He thereupon immediately told a fellow employee as well as Mike about his encounter in the house that night. Dave became so shaken by the memory of these events that he asked his brother to return to the house with him and sleep over.

Mike agreed and *slept in the spare bedroom just as I had seen him during the OBE I underwent that night!* The mystery of my puzzling observation now seemed solved, which certainly comforted me no end.

The events of August 22 ended the mini-haunting. Dave assured me that he heard none of the now-familiar raps or moans at any time after that date. This quiescence lasted until August 30, which was the day I *physically* returned home. So the total duration of the haunting would have been August 8 through August 22, inclusively.

Now there are three major parallels between the haunting/poltergeist-type phenomena that Dave Ostovich reported to me, and the OBEs I was simultaneously undergoing while in New York. These correspondences certainly lead me to believe that there was a definite connection between this "haunting" and my own unusual experiences.

To begin with, the haunting/poltergeist in my home was presumably only active between August 8 through August 22, and abruptly ceased after that. This is a curious coincidence indeed! Second, during at least one of my OBEs I had the strong urge to make my presence known to Dave. And *this* was on the night of Dave's most vivid experience. Note, too, that during my OBEs I always found myself walking up or down the hallway of my house. I do not recall any experience during which I moved about in any other part of the house. (Although I did, on occasion, walk into the bedrooms that adjoin the hall.) Now this was the very same location where Dave saw the apparition on August 22. This was also the date on which I saw Mike in the house sleeping in the spare bedroom while I was "visiting" out-of-body. I had no normal reason to expect Mike to be staying at the house that night, so the fact that I correctly saw him sleeping in the spare bedroom strikes me as extremely evidential.

I should add at this point that Mike independently informed me that he had slept over on the night of August 22 before I told him about my OBE experiences or, for that matter, anything else about what had happened in New York. So I in no way led him by any questions into misrecalling the date.

The idea that I was actually responsible for this rash of disturbances, produced while in an out-of-body state, therefore seems a likely solution to this mysterious and short-lived haunting/poltergeist.

Despite these correspondences, though, there are some peculiarities about the case that must also be kept in mind. While in New York, I always retired between 11:15 and 11:30 P.M.. This doesn't exactly jibe with Dave's experiences, which usually began around 6:30 in the evening in Los Angeles. This would only have been 9:30 P.M. in New York. In fact, Dave claimed that the *first* haunting phenomena he witnessed occurred when I would still have been aboard my plane heading for New York! This would indicate that either I had some type of OBEs that I never consciously became aware of while I was still awake, or that there was a curious disturbance in time as well as space during my OBEs. One could probably make a strong case for either of these theories, but trying to figure out the cause of these discrepancies would be too cumbersome to undertake at this time.

I personally have no predilection toward either theory. The important thing is that the poltergeist and my own OBE experiences during this rather bizarre sequence of events were interrelated in a huge psi-complex or nexus.

It is, of course, hard to draw any solid conclusions from this series of events, but it certainly does seem possible that some poltergeists can be projected at a distance by the living. Thus, they may not always result from the aggressions of a hostile but repressed adolescent. I certainly do not fit easily the criteria of the poltergeist "personality," but I apparently produced one nonetheless. My experiences also lead me to believe that at least some haunted houses are really "disguised" poltergeist cases in that they are really being produced—like the poltergeist—by the witnesses themselves, or at least by a living agent.

9

New Light on the Poltergeist

When I first entered parapsychology back in the late 1960s, the "repressed hostility" factor was the only clue we had toward solving the poltergeist mystery. The idea that poltergeists originated from projected repressions was a neat, encompassing, and testable theory. You merely had to go out into the field, find a genuine case, localize the probable agent, and then give him or her a battery of psychological tests. This was the basic procedure poltergeist investigators began employing both in this country and in Europe, and they are still using it today. The protocol worked rather well, too, and several cases supporting the repressed hostility theory soon came to light. The findings were so consistent that no one ever bothered to question them. The mystery of the poltergeist appeared to be solved.

Belief in this general theoretical model carried forward well into the 1970s. It was so widely adopted that it became almost a dogma within parapsychology. For example, Dr. Carroll B. Nash (a biologist and parapsychologist at St. Joseph's College in Philadelphia) cited the theory in 1978 as a literal fact in his textbook, *Science of Psi.* The text states that "individuals who are centers of poltergeist activity are not conscious of their causal relationship to the paranormal phenomena, and tests have indicated that they possess hostility which cannot be expressed in normal ways. The production of poltergeist phenomena permits expression of the hostility without the individual feeling responsible for it." Similar quotes and sentiments could be extracted from several other books on parapsychology published during the 1960s, 1970s, and even the 1980s.

Parapsychologists, including myself, cannot really be criticized for the way we adopted this theory so eagerly as a total explanation for the poltergeist. The discovery of a consistent pattern of repressed and denied hostility in the focal agents generating these cases was simply too overt a clue not to leap upon. It solved a mystery long puzzling poltergeist experts, and it certainly explained the poltergeist better than any prior theories had.

For years, parapsychologists had realized that the poltergeist liked to focus its unwelcomed attentions on psychologically disturbed people. But the specific dynamics of this pattern of disturbance remained annoyingly elusive. Back in the 1920s and 1930s, sexual conflicts were blamed for the poltergeist. Puberty was considered prime poltergeist season, but this idea was eventually scrapped when it became clear that not all poltergeist agents were going through this important change in their lives. The projected repression theory, first formally presented in the 1940s and 1950s, came into vogue as an extension to these earlier speculations. The development of sophisticated psychological-testing techniques after the Second World War fueled the psychodynamic study of the poltergeist. So when W. G. Roll and Dr. Hans Bender began their poltergeist hunts in the 1960s, they of course drew upon this rapidly developing prototechnology within clinical psychology and psychiatry. When they began confirming that poltergeist agents suffered from specific psychological dysfunctions, other parapsychologists hopped aboard the bandwagon. The result was that other theoretical approaches to the poltergeist were either forgotten or simply ignored. For example, when Raymond Bayless suggested in his book *The Enigma of the Poltergeist* (1967) that some poltergeists might have more complex causes and roots, his ideas were simply ignored. (His book wasn't even reviewed in a single major parapsychology journal.) Parapsychology had once again proved that it could champion rationality by naturalizing the supernatural, and any renewed attempt to reimbue the poltergeist with mystery seemed untenable or intolerable.

Despite this state of affairs, not everyone within the parapsychological community was completely sold on the repressed hostility theory as a *total* solution to the poltergeist mystery. When I published my own first major evaluation of the poltergeist in 1979, I adopted the theory with some reservation.* Although the evidence supporting the theory was impressive, there were still some problems with the model as an all-encompassing explanation. I therefore wrote:

> I also have to admit that I have doubts about putting too much stock in the "projected repression" theory. Perhaps this is really only a contributing factor leading to the outbreak of the poltergeist. It might not be the primary cause. In many cases investigators have been dealing with young children or adolescents on the verge of adulthood. I wonder: if you gave psychological tests to the next ten teenagers you met on the street, how many of them would reveal the strong use of repression and denial in their test results? It comes right down to the "how big is big?" paradox. Since we have no baselines to judge how much denial and repression is normally used by an average teen-ager or young adult, we cannot accurately state how atypical [some poltergeist] agents really are. Are they truly different from the "normal" teen-ager coping with today's troubled times?

> There can be little doubt that the repression of hostility from conscious expression is a true characteristic of the poltergeist agent, but the poltergeist is just not that simple. Denied frustration seems to be a catalyzing cause, but not the primary causative ingredient of the poltergeist. Cases of poltergeists born from "projected repression" obviously do exist, but they are only a portion of the total picture . . .

---

*The Poltergeist Experience (New York: Penguin, 1979).

I still maintain this view today. Some poltergeists created through the massive denial and repression of anger and aggression no doubt exist. But other types of poltergeists, generated by quite different causative factors, probably exist as well. By 1979 I felt that it was about time to begin examining these other types of cases in more depth. I began this project subtly in my *The Poltergeist Experience,* and I have designed this current volume as a more complete statement.

I don't mean to sound like an isolated voice in the wilderness, however. While I was busy presenting my rather nonconformist opinions, other poltergeist investigators were beginning to present similar views. The most vocal of these came from across the ocean, when Dr. Alan Gauld and Dr. A. D. Cornell came out with their own major reevaluation of the poltergeist in 1979. Their fascinating book *Poltergeists* actually rejects the psychological approach to the poltergeist as inherently superficial. While writing about their personal experiences with a poltergeist holding forth in the east Midlands, for example, they state that they found the probable agent perfectly normal. They explain that the teenaged boy ". . . did not strike us as being in any way psychologically abnormal." They add that "we found no evidence that his family life was not happy and he himself well-adjusted to it. We did not feel inclined to plant in his or his mother's mind the idea that he might not be quite normal by suddenly subjecting him to a battery of psychology tests (in the value of which we had in any case little faith)."

These are not the views of two naive "ghost hunters" either, since Dr. Gauld is a lecturer in psychology at the University of Nottingham. Their brief comments actually place into perspective two challenges to the projected repression theory. First they deny that all poltergeist cases will conform to this pattern. But second and more importantly, they suggest that *the psychological tests traditionally used to substantiate this theory are themselves invalid.* This is a surprising and crucial criticism, for repressed hostility has traditionally been documented through the use of such tests. But if the validity of these tests falters, so does the theory about the nature of the poltergeist that they support. It is certainly no understatement to say that the development, implementation, and interpretation of many psychological tests is rarely a cut-and-dried matter. This issue has not been lost to at least a few students of the poltergeist.

Some researchers interested in this problem have recently begun to critically analyze the very tests usually employed during conventional poltergeist fieldwork. In 1980, Alfonso Martinez Taboas and Carlos S. Alvarado (two researchers originally from Puerto Rico) began issuing a series of critical papers on this subject. Their views and conclusions have become more controversial than I could ever dream of mine becoming! For example, Mr. Martinez Taboas has recently written that "the psychopathological model of RSPK phenomena has been based on flimsy evidence and inadequate diagnoses, and is replete with obvious pitfalls which make it impossible for the critical researcher to evaluate properly its validity and usefulness." These views resulted when he and Alvarado started analyzing the way in which psychological testing has been employed to substantiate the repressed hostility model.

Martinez Taboas and Alvarado begin their line of argumentation by pointing out that about 50 percent of the general population will reveal some minor psychological problems when given psychodiagnostic psychological tests. So from a purely psychological standpoint, they argue, many people who are *not* poltergeist agents are just as disturbed as those rare individuals who are. They therefore argue that poltergeist victims are not then *uniquely* disturbed. But the two researchers do not stop there, for they also take issue with the specific psychological tests usually employed by poltergeist investigators. Most of these tests are not truly objective, since the person taking them merely offers open-ended responses to the test material—such as interpreting an ink-blot, completing a sentence, or making up a story about a series of ambiguous pictures. The psychologist interpreting these responses will similarly base his or her evaluations on both a few guiding principles mixed in with a great deal of "clinical instinct."* Now this is the process that Martinez Taboas and Alvarado find so unsatisfactory. They point out that these types

---

*The tests I employed during my investigation of the Dell case (see Chapter 7) are typical of these projective tests. They included having the subject draw figures, complete sentences, and interpret a series of cartoon scenes.

of tests (called "projective tests" in psychology) do not provide the clinician with data that can be objectively evaluated. The psychologist presented with data culled from these tests will be automatically predisposed to see patterns of pathology if he or she is led to expect it. The two researchers further point out that several experimental studies have objectively shown that such a process often complicates the application of psychological testing. It's all rather like the joke about the psychiatrist who liked to diagnose his patients on the basis of how they showed up for their appointments. Patients who were early were diagnosed as anxiety-ridden; those who were late were considered resistant. As for those who showed up right on time, well, obviously they were compulsive!

Mr. Martinez Taboas and Mr. Alvarado rightly feel that these findings and principles are directly pertinent to poltergeist research. The psychologists brought in to evaluate most poltergeist agents have usually been briefed about the situations that they are evaluating. Many of them have, in fact, been psychologists already interested in the poltergeist. It is not difficult to believe that these clinicians could have been biased to see pathology in the agent's test results even when none really existed.

But another factor complicates the picture as well. Both Mr. Martinez Toboas and Mr. Alvarado argue that some of the tests traditionally used to evaluate poltergeist agents are themselves suspect. They especially single out the Rorschach Test and the Thematic Apperception Test (in which the subject tells stories about a series of twenty cartoon scenes). These two tests have often been used by poltergeist researchers, yet the validity of these tests has not gone unchallenged. To build a strong case for their views, Martinez Taboas and Alvarado point to a paper by J. Zubin published in R. L. Spitzer and D. F. Klein's *Critical Issues in Psychiatric Diagnosis*. The noted psychopathologist observes in his evaluation that "the use of individual signs of psychopathology in the form of specific Rorschach, TAT, and [Draw-a-Person] responses is not a valid procedure for making inferences regarding the presence of psychopathology." Evaluations of the construct validity of such projective tests have sometimes fared rather poorly as well.

It is important to note that neither Mr. Martinez Taboas nor Mr. Alvarado are specifically trying to debunk the repressed hostility theory. Their primary goal is simply to show that this theory has not been adequately tested or documented. They also feel that it has been prematurely adopted by parapsychologists. Mr. Martinez Taboas has summed up his position rather well in some of his more recent papers. In a recent issue of the *Journal of the American Society for Psychical Research* he stated, "the psychopathological model has not been investigated until now in a rigorous and scientific way. Clinical impressions, non-blind judgments, and dubious tests are not adequate or sufficient evidence to sustain this model, or any other one."

What is perhaps the most surprising outcome of such statements is how *little* impact they have made on parapsychologists. It is certainly revealing that no one has replied to these charges in any detail. Mr. Martinez Taboas and Mr. Alvarado have presented their criticism in one form or another in the *Parapsychology Review*, the *European Journal of Parapsychology*, and the *Journal of the American Society for Psychical Research*. No considered and detailed responses have been made to their charges even though these journals are read by all parapsychologists actively engaged in parapsychological research today. It would seem that either poltergeist researchers are indifferent to this sort of critical reexamination of their favorite theories, or that parapsychologists just aren't very interested in poltergeists. The only exception came in 1982 when I felt compelled to publish some informal criticisms of the Martinez Taboas/Alvarado claims in the *European Journal of Parapsychology*. My response revolved around three issues central to their criticisms:

1. *The high level of psychopathology found within the general public is irrelevant to the issue of whether poltergeist agents are pathologically disturbed.* No one can deny that a good many people in the world today suffer from their own idiosyncratic neuroses and pathological traits. There are, however, dozens upon dozens of disorders, trait disturbances, and other patterns of pathology codified and described in the official diagnostic manual used in psychiatry today. What we find when we look at poltergeist agents is a *specific* *pattern* of psychopathology—that is, denied and repressed levels of overwhelming anger and aggression. Neither Mr. Martinez Taboas nor Carlos Alvarado has provided us with any evidence that this pattern is widespread within the general public.

  2. *"Blind" and therefore objective evaluations of poltergeist agents have, in fact, documented the role repressed hostility plays in some outbreaks.* Two such cases have so far been placed in the literature. The first was reported in 1974 by Dr. John Palmer who was then a researcher at the University of Virginia. The case took place in a small southern town, and the events focused on a ten-year-old boy. Psychological testing was performed by a psychologist who had no interest in poltergeist research, nor did she know that she was dealing with a poltergeist agent. She nonetheless isolated a clear pattern of repressed hostility while examining the boy. I also pointed to my official report on the Dell family's poltergeist (see Chapter 7). To study the dynamics of this case, I asked Dr. Gertrude Schmeidler to blindly evaluate psychological test data procured from all the pertinent family members living in the poltergeist-ridden house. She, too, spotted evidence of psychological repression in the material sent to her.

  It should be noted that this report sparked a short controversy between Mr. Martinez Taboas and me in the journal where it was originally published. My worthy opponent claimed that Dr. Schmeidler probably knew about my theory that some poltergeists are family-generated and therefore do not revolve around a central agent. His point was that she might have been biased to present me with evidence in keeping with my views. My reply was that such an explanation for the results of Dr. Schmeidler's evaluation was totally speculative, especially since I did not tell my colleague that we were dealing with a likely family poltergeist. In fact, I had specifically told her that none of the responses I was sending came from the primary agent in the case. This was of course technically true, since I didn't believe there *was* one single agent in the case. But my instructions to Dr. Schmeidler also constituted a surreptitious ploy to misdirect her bias *away* from bogusly reading pathology into the results. Nonetheless, evidence of pathological disturbances was so clear in the Dell family that she had no problem spotting it.

3. *Formal and objective evidence of repressed hostility is not really needed in some cases.* While I have great professional regard for both Mr. Martinez Taboas and Mr. Alvarado, the fact remains that neither of these critics has had much practical experience dealing with poltergeist cases. They are primarily arm-chair critics of the repressed hostility theory. On the other hand, many of my personal views have been based on my own field experience. I can assure you that when confronting a poltergeist-ridden family, psychological tests aren't usually needed to see what's going on. The patterns of pathology and repressed hostility are often so incredibly overt that formal psychological testing becomes superfluous. I can remember investigating one case in which I was afraid that the central agent was going to physically attack one of the other family members; that's how tense the situation had become. But when I asked this troubled teenager why she was so hostile toward her relative, she totally denied harboring the slightest resentment toward her! It certainly didn't take the TAT or a Rorschach ink-blot to tell me what was happening in this poorly communicating and embittered family.

I should add, however, that I agree with both Mr. Martinez Taboas and Mr. Alvarado on two issues. The repressed hostility theory has been too readily adopted by parapsychologists, even though it is obviously applicable to some cases. That the formal objective evidence substantiating this theory could and *should* be better is not an issue of contention between us, either.

These two points of agreement led me, in fact, to also suggest that we should be critically reevaluating how we employ psychological testing in our poltergeist investigations. These suggestions were made to the 1983 convention of the Parapsychological Association held at Fairleigh Dickinson University in Madison, New Jersey. My proposal centered around dispensing with projective tests entirely, and using instead a subscale drawn from the Minnesota Multiphasic Personality Inventory (MMPI). This test is one of the most frequently used diagnostic aids in psychology, and it consists of over 500 questions that can be answered simply yes or no. The results are usually computer scored. The subscale that so ignited my interest is actually one used in criminology to isolate people who overcontrol their hostility. The "overcontrolled" hostile type is psychodynamically similar to our traditional view of the poltergeist agent. Dr. Donald Lunde, an expert on criminal psychiatry, has described the overcontrolled hostile type as someone who has "developed unusually strong inhibitions against the expression of aggression in any form. Even socially approved outlets for aggression, such as profanity or a punching bag, are found to be off-limits." These people repress their hostility until they reach a breaking point. The inhibiting mechanisms built into their psyches then give away completely, the result being a wild act of violence or a spree of violent acts.

It should be pretty obvious how this profile fits in with the characteristics that usually define the "poltergeist" personality. One would predict that such a person would score above the mean on this scale. Because poltergeist agents are sometimes not aware of their complicity in the events taking place around them, it would perhaps be best if MMPI data could be collected from several such agents. Some sort of group assessment could then be made. Poltergeist agents might conceivably score less robustly on this scale than actual criminals, so more data might be required to show a statistically significant effect.

Since making this proposal, I have been actively attempting to use it in my own work. I was able to find two poltergeist cases already published in the literature where MMPI data had been taken from the primary agents, but I was unable to procure copies of their responses. The Tucson rock-throwing case gave me an opportunity to use the MMPI, but the results were contaminated by some problems in the way two of the family members answered the questionnaire. I am hopeful, though, that other poltergeist researchers will be willing to use this test during their own investigations. I will be curious to see how it fares as a method for isolating the psychodynamics of the poltergeist.

But now what about the epilepsy connection? In the first chapter of this book, I pointed out that there were two commonly proposed models for explaining the poltergeist. The first was the repressed hostility theory, which we have just been evaluating. This approach to the poltergeist has recently been superceded by a more psychophysiological one, although the two models are not mutually contradictory. They have, in fact, been both championed by W. G. Roll, who has been instrumental in popularizing them. Recently, though, Mr. Roll has been placing more emphasis on this newer approach.

Being first alerted to a possible connection between epilepsy and the poltergeist through his Michigan case of 1975, the results of some further research led him to wholeheartedly endorse the epilepsy/CNS (central nervous system) disturbance theory a few years later. There were two primary reasons for Roll's reoriented approach to the poltergeist. The first came when he began digging out the EEG data that he had collected from several agents involved in some of his earlier cases. Some of these teenagers showed odd spikes in their EEGs indicative of epilepsy or of epileptic predisposition. Roll was further encouraged to believe he was onto something when he made a detailed examination of 116 historical poltergeist cases described in the literature. There he found evidence that the agents in some of these cases might have been suffering CNS disturbances. Specific poltergeist agents had been isolated in 92 of the cases, and many of them—from the accounts left by the primary witnesses—could well have been suffering from a gamut of CNS and related medical problems. Some were even formally diagnosed as epileptic.

These various lines of support led Roll to conclude that,

> . . . a small but significant proportion of RSPK agents have been diagnosed as suffering from the sudden and recurrent disturbances of the central nervous system known as epilepsy and many others show mental and behavioral characteristics suggestive of epilepsy or have problems which may bring on CNS disturbances. In view of the fact that it is only in recent years that we have paid much attention to the health of the RSPK agent and that the reports usually emphasize descriptions of the phenomena rather than the characteristics of the central person, it is highly suggestive, in my opinion, that as many as 22 of the 92 agents were reported

on one or more occasions to have seizures, comas, etc, or to
be prone to dissociative episodes, while another 27 had
other medical or psychological problems, some of which
may be associated with CNS dysfunction.

Roll didn't wish to be too rash in drawing these conclusions, and
he did not overgeneralize from his findings.*

He points out that the CNS theory does not imply that all
epileptics will become poltergeist agents, but he adds:

> The CNS eruptions which result in familiar forms of
> epilepsy do not necessarily also result in RSPK. In the same
> way as CNS disturbances may bring on myoclonic seizures
> and no other epileptic symptoms, so CNS disturbances may
> result only in RSPK and not in any of the familiar epileptic
> symptoms. The theory also does not suppose that all pol-
> tergeist agents suffer from familiar forms of epilepsy.

The link between the poltergeist and CNS disturbances may
seem rather convincing at first. But hold on a minute, for Alfonso
Martinez Taboas has subjected this possibility to the same critical
scrutiny he originally offered the repressed hostility theory. He
points out, for instance, that there was no overt connection between the CNS disturbances and the RSPK in some cases where
the poltergeist agent in the recorded cases was obviously epileptic. The linkup may simply have been coincidental in these instances. (The close connection between Peter Mueller's epilepsy
and the raps heard during Roll's 1975 Michigan investigation
would seem to be an exception to this rule.) Mr. Martinez Taboas
has also taken issue with Roll's claim that the clinical EEGs of
some suspected poltergeist agents show spikes indicative of an
undiagnosed problem. The Puerto Rican researcher points out
that spikes or paroxysmal abnormalities occur 15 to 25 percent
of the time when EEGs are taken from normal children. Bursts
of such spikes, he continues, are typical of adult EEGs as well. But
what seems to really annoy Martinez Taboas is the way in which

---

*For some historical notes on the link between epilepsy and the poltergeist, refer
to Appendix I.

Roll has extended the support basis for his theory. Roll believes that, with some poltergeist agents, a host of symptoms apart from actual seizures might be pointing to CNS or epileptic problems. Within this category he places hyperactivity, recurrent headaches and nausea, sensory hallucinations, déjà-vu experiences, sudden bursts of fear or rage, and so on. Although some of these symptoms are often linked to specific forms of epilepsy, Martinez Taboas feels that Roll has gone overboard in assuming that they invariably result from CNS problems.

My own feeling on the issue is that both Roll and his detractor have some valid points to make. The latter has made an excellent point by arguing that no direct and predictable link between epilepsy, CNS disturbances, and the poltergeist has been found. On the other hand, Roll's 1975 Michigan case perfectly substantiates the existence of an epilepsy/poltergeist relationship. The existence of even one such case of this sort compels us to take the poltergeist/CNS disturbance theory seriously. It certainly serves as a clue that we should be following up.

So after all these points and counterpoints, where do we stand? Can parapsychology today explain the poltergeist or can't it? My own answer is that parapsychology seems well on its way toward understanding the poltergeist, but we must be careful not to generalize or oversimplify the matter. The simple fact remains that *different poltergeist cases emerge from different psychological roots.* It is as simple as that. This is not to say that poltergeist cases generated by repressed hostility do not exist or are relatively rare. They definitely represent a common subtype of RSPK outbreak. It is equally possible that some cases may be linked to psychophysiological quirks in the agent's central nervous system, though I am personally far from sure whether the RSPK or the epileptic symptoms came first in these cases. The only thing that bothers me is the habit some researchers have in trying to fit each and every poltergeist case they come across into one or the other of these molds.

The fact that some poltergeist cases may have rather offbeat causes is especially true of cases that break out in cultures other than our own. For example, fear of witchcraft and black magic is common among the working classes of Brazil. So it isn't surprising to find many poltergeist cases erupting within Brazilian families who were recently "cursed" by a neighbor or enemy. It is, however, the fear of the curse that is probably causing the eruptions in these cases, not the curses or magical acts themselves. We are therefore faced with the curious paradox that, at least in some cultures, fear of the poltergeist is a common way of conjuring one into existence!

If you now go back to the several cases that I've personally examined and studied, it seems clear that wholly different etiologies must be posited to explain just about each of them. The following "solutions" to the cases presented in Chapters 2 through 8 tend to remind us of the great diversity of the poltergeist.

THE 1974 LOS ANGELES POLTERGEIST

This case presents an almost classic example of the common "adolescent" poltergeist, the very sort upon which the repressed hostility theory has been traditionally based. The case supports this model since Chris, the focal agent, was obviously denying and repressing huge amounts of hostility. During the three days I remained in the house, the interfamily tension was enormous. Bouts of verbal violence finally broke out as the poltergeist finally ebbed. The roots of Chris's hostility ran deep and were focused on the stepfather who had deserted her, the grandmother who was invading her relationship with her mother, and toward her newly born infant sister.

There were other factors that complicated the case as well. It was once believed that sexual conflicts were the cause of most poltergeist outbreaks, but this theory went out of style after the Second World War. Sexual overtones have nonetheless played a prominent role in at least a few contemporary accounts.* Chris's disturbed sexual development played an obvious role in her pathology. This was, no doubt, due to her premature development.

---

*Dolls, for instance, were placed in lewd positions by the Nickleheim poltergeist which I discussed in Chapter 1.

Her attitude toward her own attractiveness was apparently ambivalent. She was often openly seductive, yet avoided going to
school because of the sexual taunts of her classmates. It is also
revealing that she eventually escaped the poltergeist and her
home life by running away and living with a migrant worker who
thought she was eighteen. (She was actually only fourteen at the
time.) There were other indications that Chris was troubled by
sexual conflicts, but it would be a violation of confidence to go
into them here.

THE FIRE POLTERGEIST IN SIMI VALLEY

For this case I can offer no solution since I was never able to
locate and talk with the young man who was the likely agent. The
more I spoke with Mr. Eaton, the more I came to the conclusion
that he was probably *not* the cause of the fires—either normally
or paranormally. Since he had known his young visitor only very
briefly, he could offer no insights about his private life or living
situation.

THE ELECTRONIC POLTERGEIST IN
HOLLYWOOD

This strange case partially supports the repressed hostility theory, although the fit is a bit procrustean. Mrs. Gladys Gordon was
the obvious source of the gremlins haunting the factory where
she worked, and she knew it. So did everyone else who worked
there. Like so many other more traditional poltergeist agents,
Ms. Gordon was suffering some major problems in her private
life, including her rather ambivalent attitude toward her personal
relationship with her boss. She was in a sense trapped by these
problems since she could foresee no practical solution to them.
She also came to realize that the electronic disturbances in the
factory and in her home seemed to correlate with the times when
she was under the most pressure.

Despite all of these factors, it would not be correct to say
that the case derived strictly from the agent's repressed hostility.

Ms. Gordon was well aware of her feelings, and she was able to articulate them rather well. Unlike so many (primarily young) poltergeist agents, she was a very insightful and intelligent woman. Her poltergeist problem arose from a conflict for which there was no solution, not from anger or aggression per se. So while her problem resulted from psychological roots, the much overworked repressed hostility theory doesn't quite cover it. Her emotions may have been pent up, but not truly repressed.

TUCSON'S ROCK-THROWING POLTERGEIST

From the standpoint of psychodynamic theory, this case probably represents the most puzzling one I've ever confronted. The setting of the case was fairly typical for the poltergeist in general, since it revolved around a middle-class family that included a number of teenaged children. It quickly became apparent to me, however, that this family didn't conform in any way to your typically disturbed poltergeist family. Everyone was mutually giving, understanding, affectionate, and they all communicated well with one another. The Berkbiglers were so obviously normal that I was at first tempted to believe that the stones really *were* being thrown by a prankster. Only my subsequent observations proved to the contrary.

By the end of my investigation, the only clue I was able to uncover about the case was young David's complaint about the foul odors. The olfactory phenomenon is classically produced by anomalous neural firing in the brain's temporal lobes. My first impression was, therefore, that this case supported Roll's contention that poltergeists may be expressing CNS dysfunctions. There were, however, two problems with this solution to the case. Since David's symptom started bothering him only *after* the rock-throwings had already begun, we are confronted with a chicken/egg paradox. Did the temporal lobe problem produce the poltergeist, or vice versa? It should also be kept in mind that David, like his fellow family members, had often been hit by the flying rocks. Even a minor injury to the head could cause the emergence of a temporal lobe symptom.

I found myself baffled by this case for several months until a friend of mine suggested a possible solution. During a workshop I gave on the Tucson case in Dallas in 1984, Patric Giesler —a young anthropologist at the Institute for Parapsychology in Durham, North Carolina—came up with some fresh insights on the case. He pointed out that the rock-throwings began when the Berkbiglers, already suspicious that a vagrant had been living in their uncompleted structure, first moved into their new home. He rightfully suggested that the family may have been expecting some sort of trouble. The poltergeist then wreaked havoc for ten weeks straight until the very day that a mysterious prowler (who was no doubt a sheriff's official) was chased off the property. Patric suggested to me that this poltergeist may have been caused by the family's own fears, expectations, and beliefs. They may have psychically conjured into existence the very "prankster" they were expecting. This novel theory can also explain why the poltergeist *only* produced phenomena attributable to a prankster —that is, the rock-throwings and the poundings on the front door during the first week of the disturbance.

This general theory may strike you as rather offbeat, but there is considerable evidence that could be marshalled in support of it. Patric himself based his explanation on the theories and research of Kenneth Batcheldor, a British psychologist actively involved in the study of psychokinesis. Batcheldor has studied the phenomenon of paranormal table-tilting for years, usually in the dark but under conditions of some experimental control. He has found that the best way to get the PK going is to deliberately (though secretly) shove the table manually. The real PK will often pick up right afterward. The British psychologist calls this phenomenon "artifact induction," and he believes that it works because of its impact on the belief-systems of the sitters. First having been fooled by the bogus effect, the sitters can now overcome their own skepticism and resistance, thereby becoming free to produce their own (genuine) effects. Patric suggested to me that a similar process might have produced the Tucson stone-throwings—that is, the belief that a prankster was on their property may have led the Berkbiglers into paranormally creating one. The fact that food had been found missing from the refrigerator before the poltergeist arrived might have served as the "artifact."

The notion that a poltergeist infestation can be engendered by expectancy and artifact is of course speculative. But it represents a novel and potentially promising approach to this most puzzling case . . . a case that seems to resist more conventional explanations.

THE ROSES' ODORIFEROUS POLTERGEIST

Pent-up hostility that couldn't find a normal outlet of expression certainly played a role in the Roses' little poltergeist problem. This troubled, harried, and tormented family was being persecuted by their relatives, threatened with black magic, and stuck with a stinky ghost to boot. The specific dynamics of this case actually resemble those that you find in some cases reported from Brazil, where the fear of hexes and black magic can bring about a poltergeist. To find such a case reported from our own culture is quite extraordinary, however.

It could be argued that pent-up aggression and anger was the sole cause of this minor case, but note once again how the dynamics of the Rose case differ from the usual pattern of repressed hostility so often linked with the poltergeist. The emotions underlying the disturbances were directed at an outside source and didn't represent an interfamily one. Nor was the hostility being repressed. The Roses knew that they had a sizable problem on their hands. The tragedy—as well as the cause of the poltergeist—was simply that they did not know how to deal with or resolve it. Blocked channels of communication also probably played a role in this case as well.

A TALKING POLTERGEIST IN LOS ANGELES

The problem Mrs. Thomas found herself facing in her modest downtown home was rather difficult for us to evaluate, since the case seemed to be a composite of both a haunting and a poltergeist. We were able to uncover some evidence that Mrs. Thomas was harboring conflicts over her work and living situation. So in this sense, the case could provide provisional support for the repressed hostility theory. I prefer, however, to consider this case unsolved. Neither Raymond Bayless nor I saw any evidence that Mrs. Thomas was psychologically disturbed or even overly unhappy. She seemed to be dealing with the same problems most middle-class people so often confront in this dog-eat-dog world of ours. No one else in her small family appeared to be the agent in the case either.

MR. CECCATO'S LIFELONG POLTERGEIST

The situation we found with Alfred Ceccato and his young family is altogether different from any of the other cases recounted in this volume. There were no communication blocks disrupting their interactions, no evidence of repressed emotions, no tensions, and certainly no epilepsy. Because of his long history of running into hauntings and poltergeists, it seems clear that Mr. Ceccato simply possesses an excess amount of psychic ability. For some reason this ability has a tendency to express itself spontaneously. The result has been periodic PK eruptions in the various homes where he and his family have resided.

THE DELLS' FAMILY POLTERGEIST

The Dell case fits quite well into our more conventional view of the poltergeist. Here we had a very disturbed family—complete with interfamily tensions, drug abuse, runaways, as well as several other evidences of an unhappy home. Faced with such a range of psychological stress and dysfunction, it shouldn't seem odd that something just had to give. The poltergeist that was haunting their apartment was merely one expression of the family's unconscious cries for help. Probably the only atypical feature of this case was that no particular person in the household could be identified as the focal agent. The poltergeist appeared to be jointly created by the entire family. This in no way detracts, however, from the fact that the poltergeist was a bundle of projected repression.

In fact, this case can be totally explained on the repressed hostility theory. Each of the family members possessed typical characteristics of the "classic" poltergeist agent. Psychological testing showed that Terri, the teenaged daughter, possessed absolutely no threshold for frustration, while both her parents tended to deny and repress their aggressions and hostility. This might not be a very pretty picture, but it certainly explains why a poltergeist erupted in their home.

MY OWN OUT-OF-BODY POLTERGEIST

Once again this case falls into an entirely different category from the other cases presented in this book. This small-scale psychic infestation was not related to anyone truly living in the house. The paranormal events were "sent" there, so to speak, by me from a city thousands of miles away. It was sort of an "experimental" poltergeist.

The idea that someone can "send" a poltergeist to an enemy or to a second party is full of fascinating implications. If such a process really works, it would force us to reconsider many of those cases (such as those reported from South America) where poltergeist attacks have resulted from black magic practices. Most of these outbreaks are no doubt due to the victims' own fears upon learning that magic is being used against them. Yet perhaps under rare circumstances a poltergeist can actually be sent by one person to another. The fact remains that several cases of similar out-of-body poltergeists have been placed in the literature. (Please refer to Appendix II for a description of some of these cases.) Although these cases are probably telling us more about the mechanics of the poltergeist than the psychological principles behind them, the implications that can be drawn from such reports are far-reaching.

With all these summaries and reconsiderations in mind, what conclusions can we reach about the poltergeist? It seems pretty clear to me that, to begin with, the cases with which I've been so personally involved do not really substantiate the two most commonly proposed *universal* explanations for the poltergeist. Only two of my cases clearly support the repressed hostility theory, while only one of them offers any support for the epilepsy/CNS hypothesis. Several of my cases indicate that psychological *conflicts* can generate a poltergeist, but this is a far cry from saying that repressed hostility is the particular cause of most outbreaks. The other cases I've investigated either defy solution or were caused by rather bizarre circumstances.

So I guess the only thing we can say about poltergeists in general is that they seem to be produced by us, the living. The older view that these attacks were caused by demons or spirits of the dead seems rather simplistic, though I would not rule out even this possibility for some cases described in the literature.

I would once again like to point out, though, that nothing I am saying in this chapter contradicts the findings of other parapsychologists who have studied the poltergeist. My feeling is that such researchers as W. G. Roll here in the United States and Dr. Hans Bender in Germany have simply and repeatedly stumbled across a specific type of poltergeist. It does appear likely that poltergeists produced by repressed emotions are probably the most common type of infestation. But the existence of these cases does not rule out cases of poltergeists resulting from different factors.

My only hope is that the views I've been expressing here will serve as a warning to future poltergeist researchers. Too often those of us engaged in poltergeist research have entered into our cases with preconceived notions about what we are going to find. I am certainly guilty of this tendency, which was why I was so puzzled when I first confronted the Tucson poltergeist. The family reporting the incidents simply didn't conform to the stereotype I expected to see. The great diversity of the poltergeist and its causes suggests that we should suspend these stereotypes, or that we should hold them at bay when we start our investigations until we find good reason to resurrect them. The poltergeist simply can't be bottled, labeled, and then shelved. Each case deserves a fresh and unbiased analysis.

Nothing I am saying in this chapter should, in the long run, strike you as necessarily antiestablishment, for my own studies and field investigations really only point to one overriding principle. The poltergeist is really no more complex than the mind that gives it birth . . . though we must also remember that, paradoxically, the human mind itself represents an almost unfathomable mystery.

10

Final Notes: Some Guidelines for Investigating the Poltergeist*

Poltergeist outbreaks occur without warning, often striking deep within the domains of middle-class America. So the day may come when you will be called upon to investigate one. This is especially true if you work in the news industry or with various social service agencies, since these people are usually the first to be summoned when the activity begins. I can well remember how, when I first became interested in psychical research, the very thought of investigating a haunting or poltergeist thrilled me no end. I could hardly wait for the day when I would be asked to go out, interview the witnesses, and perhaps even witness the poltergeist myself. The cases recounted in this book indicate the extent to which this dream has come true.

Over the years I've been able to learn a great deal about *how* to investigate a poltergeist case as well. I can assure you that it is by no means an easy matter. It's a lot more complicated than

---

*Some of the suggestions presented here have been adapted from an earlier book of mine, *The Haunted House Handbook* (New York: Tempo, 1978). This material has been considerably revised to apply specifically to poltergeist cases, although some overlay was inevitable. New sections and suggestions have also been added, especially on the ethical issues arising from such field work.

just visiting the house, talking with the family members, and drinking a cup of coffee or two while waiting around for the activity to start. You really have to be shrewd. You must act somewhat like a detective while playing the role of parapsychologist, psychologist, and social worker all at the same time. You must look to find if anyone in the house has a motive for pulling a hoax; you must analyze everyone's testimony to make sure all your witnesses agree about what has been going on; and you must know what kinds of experiments to conduct in the house. But above all else, you have to develop the ability to judge character, since one of your chief duties will be to make some sort of decision about the credibility of the witnesses with whom you will be interacting.

The following guidelines will give you a very general idea about what principles and strategies are best used. These few pages are not meant to be an in-depth guide to poltergeist research, but a set of pointers on how best to handle a poltergeist should you ever confront one.

LEARNING ABOUT PROMISING CASES

There are many ways to find or at least to learn about promising cases. Probably the best thing to do is check your local papers daily and listen to the news broadcasts regularly on TV and radio. Reports about ghosts, hauntings, and poltergeists make for good back-page news stories. You will be surprised, once you start looking, how many of these strange reports find their way into print. Poltergeist reports seem to be particularly newsworthy, and I've come across some of my best cases by following the media. It was through these channels that I learned about the Simi Valley fire poltergeist and that the Psychical Research Foundation in North Carolina learned of the Tucson rock thrower. Wide coverage in the press played a prominent role in both the Bridgeport and Columbus poltergeists as well. It is also wise to make sure your friends know of your interest in this sort of research, especially if any of them work with the media or with social service agencies. I regularly receive tips from people who know of my work and alert me to promising cases.

If you come across a good story written up in the newspapers, in all likelihood the address of the house will not be listed. These stories tend to give relatively few details about the case, though the name of the puzzled family or the chief witnesses will usually be printed. So if you wish to pursue the case further, there are two courses of action open to you. Calling the police station located in the district where the case is active is probably your best bet, since families confronted by a poltergeist generally ask for help from such agencies first. (The family usually believes that a crank is responsible in some way for their problem, so this course of action is normal. Police or other law enforcement officials were called in initially in my 1974 case in Los Angeles, in the Tucson rock-throwing case, as well as in the Bridgeport and Seaford disturbances.) Police investigators and officials will usually be very helpful to you, and will often fill you in on unpublished details about the case. If you can convince them that you are not a "nut" and have a scientific interest in the poltergeist, they may even put you directly in contact with the distressed family. I've always had very good luck with the police in these situations, especially in the Tucson case where the local sheriffs bent over backwards supplying me with information.

Your second course of action would be contacting the family directly. The best way is by phone or letter. If you have the names of the witnesses but not their addresses, don't worry. Go down to your city's Hall of Records, and there you will find the addresses of anyone who has, or ever had, a telephone with a listed number. Don't forget to make use of the telephone directory as well. Sometimes the simplest method will work best.

Another good way of locating promising cases is by becoming active in a local psychical research society. Most cities have amateur clubs or groups of this nature, and very often the general public will report hauntings and poltergeists to these organizations. When I served as director of research for one such organization in Los Angeles back in 1975, promising cases trickled in all the time. These amateur groups, who usually don't have the personnel to go out and investigate all these cases, rely on volunteers to do the ground work. Your offer of assistance may very well be taken up. In fact, this is one of the ways I first got started myself.

Finally, it might also be a good idea to see if any of the faculty members at a local college or university in your hometown are interested in psychical research. (Usually they will be found in the psychology department.) Sometimes people who suddenly find themselves faced with a poltergeist will report their problems to a local university in the hope that someone there will be able to help them. These calls may be turned over to any faculty members available who have shown any interest in the field. Get to know these important contacts, since they may be willing to turn some promising cases your way.

INTERVIEWING THE WITNESSES

Your responsibility while out in the field revolves around three general tasks: (1) to determine if any normal causes can account for the disturbances; (2) to decide whether the case is genuine, a misinterpretation of normal occurrences, or a deliberate hoax; and (3) to learn all you can about the incident you are investigating. Keep remembering, however, that most of the cases you will encounter while pursuing the poltergeist will probably *not* be genuine. Many more will be infuriating mixtures of genuine effects contaminated with fraud. So one of the most important principles to keep in mind is that evidence for fraud may not be ruining your entire case. But such a discovery will alert you to be especially vigilant during your stay in the house.

Now if you want to investigate a poltergeist case seriously, your best tool-of-the-trade will be your ability to talk with and draw information from your witnesses. I rely upon interviewing witnesses more than any other method of investigation, apart from staying in the house myself in hopes of witnessing the action. By talking with all the family members involved in the case, you can sometimes learn just about everything you will need to know about the case in order to help you determine if it is authentic or not. Interviewing your witnesses is, however, no easy task.

To begin with, you should use a fairly standard procedure when collecting background material. A questionnaire for use while conducting such fieldwork has been developed at the Psychical Research Foundation, which recommends that you ascertain the following in each case you investigate:

1. Where have the disturbances taken place?
2. When did the disturbances begin?
3. How recently has anything happened?
4. How does the frequency and severity at this time compare with earlier periods?
5. Who are the members of the household or group involved? What are their ages?
6. Have any of the persons who witnessed the phenomena had telepathic dreams or other psychic experiences in the past? If so, state who they are and describe the experiences.
7. Were any of the persons who witnessed the phenomena interested in psychic matters before the present disturbances began? If so, indicate their areas of interest.
8. Have attempts been made to find an ordinary explanation of the events? For example, is there reason to think that someone is doing these things as a prank or that they could be due to settling of the house, rodents, or similar causes?
9. Are there pets or farm animals in the area? If so, how do they react to the disturbances?
10. Have any visitors to the house or area witnessed the disturbances? If so, are they willing to testify? (Give names and addresses of such persons.)
11. Do you or others who witnessed the phenomena have any idea or theory about their cause?
12. Are events more frequent at certain times during the twenty-four hours of the day than at others? If so, state which periods.
13. Are they more frequent in certain places (for example, in certain rooms of the house) than in others? If so, state where.

14. Do the occurrences happen more frequently in the presence or vicinity of certain persons than with others? If so, state which people. Do events take place when they are not in the area?

15. Has anything been known to happen when no one was in the area?

Poltergeist cases usually include violent physical displays, so your next job is to procure detailed descriptions of these incidents. The following questions are designed to ascertain if and what paranormal dimensions may be indicative of the alleged RSPK:

16. Describe these disturbances.

17. How frequent are the disturbances?

18. If there have been unexplained movements of objects, was there anything strange about the manner in which the objects moved or stopped (for example, objects that moved around corners, hit with unusually great force, and so forth)?

19. Are unusually loud noises caused by the moving of objects? If so, describe these noises.

20. Are there noises not connected with the disturbances of objects? If so, describe these noises.

21. Has anyone ever seen an object *start* to move when no one was near it? If so, describe these occurrences.

22. Have things happened when no one was in the area or room in which the disturbances took place? If so, describe the occurrences.

23. Are special objects or kinds of objects disturbed more often than others? If so, which?

These questions may seem simple and straightforward, but implementing your interview with the beleaguered family will often entail a number of problems. To begin with, there will probably be more than one or two family members who have witnessed the activity. You should not interview these people together after you get a general feel of the case. Talk to each of them about their experiences in the house privately. By following this procedure, none of the witnesses will be tempted to change his or her story to make it fit in or better correspond with the stories the others are reporting. Each witness will be forced to rely solely upon his or her own memories. Then you can go back and compare the various accounts you have received, and see whether or not they match up. As you interview your informants, it is best to have each family member relate to you the *first* odd phenomenon he or she ever encountered in the house. Then go on to the second incident, and so on. This will give you a good history of the poltergeist and not just a jumbled-up series of bizarre tales. As I said, repeat this procedure with each of the family members. After you have collected all this testimony, as well as that offered by any other witnesses, you can then start analyzing your case by asking yourself a series of questions:

Does all the testimony add up? It is important for you to make sure that all the witnesses are giving you similar accounts. If one witness claims that mysterious rappings have been heard breaking out in the house nightly, other family members should be complaining about similar manifestations. If they come up with *different* accounts about what is going on, this should alert you to the possibility that they are either making up tales or only imagining that the house is infested. I ran into this very situation right after Steven Spielberg's movie *Poltergeist* was released. A gentleman called me to say that his house was being invaded by a poltergeist and started reciting a list of phenomena that he had witnessed. These were surprisingly close to some of the effects depicted in the movie. So I merely told him to have his wife call me the next day, so that I could question her as well. (I suggested this delay so that she would call while her husband was at work and could not actively control her answers.) Sure enough, the couple hadn't rehearsed very well, and when the lady called she started describing a series of incidents drawn directly from that MGM classic movie, *The Haunting.* The ploy, so far as I was able to discern, was an act they were hoping would get them out of buying a house they couldn't afford. They were living in the house while it was still in escrow, having moved there from a less expensive section of southern California.

You should also continually ask yourself whether any of the PK has been witnessed by more than one person at the same time. If a case is genuine, usually some of the manifestations will have been collectively observed or heard, especially if the poltergeist has been particularly active. It is always best to have as many independent accounts of the *same* incident as possible. Be sure to check out these incidents carefully. If two people claim that on one occasion a fish bowl came sailing through the air, make sure both of them have described the event to you in the same way. Both witnesses, for instance, should agree on where the bowl was originally positioned in the house and the direction and speed at which it moved. If both your informants agree on these points, then you can be sure the incident actually occurred in just the way they reported it. But if they disagree, then you cannot accept the incident as evidence of anything.

Don't expect that everyone's testimony will invariably be totally consistent, though. It is a fact of human nature that some people simply have better memories and powers of observation than others. You should expect a small amount of inconsistency within your reports, but not obvious or glaring ones. That is why it is absolutely necessary for you to interview your witnesses independently.*

Now that you have all the testimony recorded, your work really begins!

First, map out the history of the case, event by event. Make sure you know the date of each incident and which family members witnessed it. You can do this by taking a sheet of paper and dividing it into three columns. In the first, give a date. Describe the incident in the second. Note in the third who was home at the time and witnessed the event as well as where he or she was located.

Proceed next by drawing up a floor plan of the house and marking off where every member of the household was standing or sitting at the time of each incident. Do this for each and every occurrence. It will become obvious to you whether the case is genuine or not as you go through this procedure. Say, for instance, that one family member reported that on one occasion a

---

*Taking down all this testimony, by the way, presents certain problems in itself. Generally, there are three ways you can record your interviews. You can make notes while talking with the family members; or have them write out detailed descriptions of their experiences; or tape record their testimony. You will probably find that taping will be the easiest and most efficient method for notetaking.

bottle came flying down the hallway stairs. Check to see where everybody else in the house was positioned at the critical moment. If everyone was sitting together in the living room when the incident occurred, it could well have been a genuine psychic event. But if everyone was in the living room except a young child —who just happened to be upstairs at the time—it is possible that this family member threw the object down the stairs.

Now check over all your maps. Check to see if one person always seems to be unaccounted for, or was by himself or herself and was unwatched whenever the PK supposedly acted up. If so, this indicates a hoax. Do not assume, however, that a case is fraudulent just because one family member always seems to be close to the disturbance or the thrown objects. There is good evidence that objects in close physical proximity to the poltergeist agent are more likely to move paranormally than more distant ones. Be sure, too, to mark off the specific trajectories of the objects. Some sort of physical principle might arise from this data, as it has in a number of poltergeist cases already placed in the literature.

If you do suspect a hoax, you can sometimes prove this to yourself just by interviewing your witnesses a little more thoroughly. See if they change their stories around. I have learned over the years that people who have experienced genuine psychic phenomena in their homes will stick to their stories no matter how hard you to try to shake them. People who are faking, or just making up tall tales, will usually try to tell you things they *think* you want to hear. So if I suspect a fraud, I will deliberately "bait" my witnesses and get them to admit to all sorts of ridiculous things! (This was one trick I used to expose the couple whose wild stories about their poltergeist followed so closely on the heels of Spielberg's *Poltergeist.* When I spoke to the husband I "suggested" to him "typical" poltergeist pranks—all of which I was making up. Sure enough his wife recited them back to me the next day!)

I have also used this trick on people who, to my knowledge, have witnessed genuine poltergeist phenomena. They have never picked up these suggestions and reported them back to me.

There are other ways you can trick a hoaxer into exposing

himself. For instance, you can get all the family members to engage in a "rap" session about what they have witnessed in the house. If your informants have not been telling you the truth, they will probably start trying to outdo each other with the best "ghost stories" they can think up. These tales can get pretty wild. I once investigated a case in which the family members originally only claimed that an apparition was stalking their house at night. It was clear from talking to them that they were just out for publicity, so I decided to have a little fun with them. I got them into a talk session, and by the end of the afternoon the claims had escalated considerably. Now they claimed that fires were being set in the house, that furniture often flew about, and that mysterious bell-like chimes and clangings were being heard all night long. The family members were trying to impress me and each other with these ridiculous stories to the point that one family member even claimed psychic levitations.

WITNESSING THE OUTBREAK

The poltergeist investigator should be equipped with all sorts of fancy gadgets while he or she is making an investigation. This is really no problem if you happen to be rich. You can, for instance, bring in cameras to continually film the house in hopes of photographing the poltergeist effects. You could even set up TV monitors to keep various rooms under constant surveillance. Dr. Hans Bender uses a version of this technique when he and his team of co-investigators are called in from Freiburg. During their work on the Nickleheim poltergeist, they used a camera setup that would keep special areas of the house continually monitored. It automated as soon as any force disturbed any of several specially located target objects placed in these areas. The plan unfortunately failed. The American Society for Psychical Research has also developed a similar mobile unit. They rarely take it out on cases, though, since they are afraid that a particularly active poltergeist might break it! Unfortunately, few poltergeist investigators are so nicely equipped; but even an amateur can at least carry out a thorough investigation without all the gadgetry.

The simplest method of actively investigating a poltergeist outbreak is to just sit and wait until something happens. If the RSPK seems to be breaking out daily, you should plan on spending some time just visiting the home. The poltergeist might go into abeyance when you first arrive, but it will sometimes make a gradual comeback. If the poltergeist is genuine, you will usually find your hosts willing to have you there, and I've stayed at such homes keeping watch for up to three days straight. While waiting to confront the poltergeist, though, you must do more than just sit around like a dead log. You must be alert at all times. You must also keep track of everyone in the house. If somebody leaves the building or walks from one room to another, you must make a written or tape-recorded note to that effect. Only by following this meticulous procedure will you be in a position to know the exact whereabouts of everyone should anything happen during your stay.

Another important rule to follow is to keep the family members under constant observation. Let's say, for instance, that an ashtray flies out of the kitchen while you are in the house. If everyone present is sitting with you in the living room, then you know that no living hand could have thrown it. But if the family members are all in different rooms—and you haven't kept track of their whereabouts—there is simply no way you can authenticate the incident.

Keeping the family under constant surveillance poses certain difficulties since you don't want to act like a kidnapper keeping check on a group of hostages. You have to be very subtle. If the family feels that you distrust them or expect fraud, they may easily become offended and ask you to leave. You could hardly blame them, either. The best way I've found to avoid this problem is to constantly engage the family members in conversation, or suggest politely that they not move around too much. People won't move about unnecessarily while you are talking with them, so I often keep up a constant chatter, encouraging my witnesses to tell me all about themselves. You might also remind the families that you are there to investigate their problem and need their full cooperation. It also helps if you happen to have a friend who is well-versed in such field work since two investigators can do the job more efficiently. It is very difficult for just one person to control and observe even a relatively small group. Over the last several years, I have always asked Raymond Bayless to accompany me on my adventures. Raymond likewise requests me to help out on his cases. We have found ourselves in a much better position to determine if a case is genuine or not by constantly monitoring different parts of the house we are investigating. Check back to my chapter on the 1974 Los Angeles poltergeist and you will see how the use of this team approach was essential to documenting it. One of the most impressive incidents of the investigation occurred during the second day of our stay. Raymond was sitting in the kitchen with two of the household members, while I was in the living room with the probable agent. Suddenly a spoon came flying out of the hallway and landed in the living room. We were thus in a perfect position to witness the incident and satisfy ourselves that it was genuinely paranormal.

If you happen to be gadget-minded, a whole realm of possibilities is open to you. You might take along thermometers and place them strategically throughout the house to see if any odd fluctuations will be recorded. You might also seal off all air vents, windows, and doors to any room which has been the scene of active disturbances and then hang mobiles from the ceiling. If any type of "psychic energy" becomes active in the room, these paper hangings may start to swing. But be very sure that no air drafts are getting into the room.

Many other suggestions for the "instrumental" study of poltergeists and haunted houses can be found by reading an article by Dr. Charles Tart of the University of California at Davis entitled "Applications of Instrumentation in the Investigation of Haunting and Poltergeist Cases." This interesting paper was published in the July 1965 issue of the *Journal of the American Society for Psychical Research.* Dr. Tart suggests how to use photocells, thermistors, tape recorders, strain gauges, and other devices in the study of such outbreaks.

ETHICAL ISSUES

During the course of my poltergeist investigations I have been forcefully impressed by how many ethical issues arise from this sort of research. When you are called in to investigate a poltergeist or haunting, the call will usually be made by an extremely distressed family; one that is usually frightened, emotionally disturbed, and is seeking—above all else—to find a way to rid themselves of their problem. The family who consults a field investigator has certain needs to which you should be sensitive. They will expect you to reduce their anxieties, educate them about what they are facing, help them cope with their problem, and do everything possible to alleviate it.

Note how a typical field investigator of an active poltergeist affords little in the way of meeting these needs. The researcher will usually rush to the spot; take a history of the case from the witnesses; and measure the trajectories of all the objects moved during the outbreak. The investigator will then usually try to discover a focal agent in the family, subject him or her to a battery of psychological tests, and will then rush to analyze the data and probably write a report on what has been learned.

Such a procedure clearly meets the needs of the parapsychologist or field investigator. But is this routine really a very ethical way of investigating such cases? Has the investigator helped the family who has invited him into their home by showing them how to deal with what they are facing? The answer to both these questions is clearly no.

Families who call in a field investigator to probe their poltergeists and hauntings do so out of fear. Always remember this cardinal point. They don't understand what is happening to them. They are terrified that spirits or demons are plaguing them, and they are usually worried that physical harm will come to them. Their chief reason for calling a parapsychologist at all is because they expect that he or she will know how to put an end to the disturbances. The one thing these families do not want—

or expect—is an investigation; nor do they want to be bullied into taking psychological tests and inventories.

The point I'm trying to make is really quite simple. When you enter into a case, you have two primary responsibilities that may sometimes conflict with each other. You certainly have a professional and scientific responsibility to investigate the case and learn as much as you can about the events in question. But you also have an even greater responsibility to spend time with the family, educate them about the nature of what they are facing, do everything possible to alleviate their fears and anxieties, and advise them about the prospects—no matter how remote—of putting an end to their difficulties. You must, in short, act as a psychotherapist. In this respect, I firmly believe that no one should conduct field investigations who does not have some background in the art of short-term psychotherapy. Knowing a little about crisis counseling and intervention helps too.

It is for this reason that my own investigations have taken on a different strategy over the years than when I first entered the field. I usually begin by asking the family for a history of their case. I then specifically ask them why they have called me, what they expect me to do about the situation, and what *they* think the cause of the disturbance is. So, before engaging in my investigation, the family is given full opportunity to explain to me what they expect me to do, and how they expect me to act. I then try to explain to them a little about the nature of the poltergeist, usually emphasizing that demons or other malicious agencies have nothing to do with such outbreaks. This will usually be the family's greatest fear, so always assure them about how relatively harmless hauntings and poltergeists are.

The lengthy process of education is meant to calm the family, answer their most obvious questions, and help them to understand the necessity for a more thorough scientific investigation. Families will not usually cooperate fully with such an investigation unless they respect what the researcher is trying to do.

If the family wishes a more thorough investigation after this process of education has been completed, several more ethical issues arise as the investigation is actually implemented. The first of these concerns whether or not the investigator should seek to

actually witness the poltergeist. This has led some field researchers to actively attempt to get the poltergeist to act up in his/her
immediate presence. This can be done by restaging the scene of
past activity or by deliberately introducing conflict into the family. This, to me, is not ethical behavior on the part of the investigator. Your chief responsibility, as I said before, is to help the
family deal with what they are confronting. If the family's major
concern is with stopping the disturbances in their home, it would
be rather unethical to deliberately encourage poltergeist activity
to act up. This is especially true if such events are bound to
frighten or cause emotional strain on the family.

The next issue you may face during such an investigation
concerns the use of psychological and/or neurophysiological
testing to help you diagnose the case. This problem is exacer-
bated if a focal agent is obviously the cause of the outbreak.

Most of us in the field view psychological testing very differ-
ently from the way these tests are viewed by members of the
general public—the very people you are likely to meet while
conducting your investigation. We view them as investigative
tools used to help gather data. However, most of your poltergeist
victims will probably view them in a radically different light. I
don't think many researchers realize just how anxiety-provoking
such testing can be.

Let me elaborate on this issue by citing a personal experience. During the course of one poltergeist case I worked on a few
years ago, I decided to give a series of psychological tests to the
family members. These were basically projective tests, but I almost undermined my own investigation by bringing them up. I
later learned that at least two of the family members believed that
the tests were meant to see if they were insane or mentally in-
competent. This ruined their trust in me as an investigator and
as someone they could turn to if the events started up again. They
also believed that the tests were a direct *assault* on their credibility
and mental health. One member even began to question his own
sanity as a result of my thoughtless use of such psychological
testing. I only realized this when the wife in the household started
calling me repeatedly to find out what the tests revealed because
her husband wanted to know if he was crazy or not.

This issue becomes even more touchy when an investigator seeks to determine if the events are focusing on a central agent. Even though this procedure is part and parcel of the usual poltergeist investigation, few researchers seem aware of the psychological ramifications that arise when such an identification has been made. Advising a family that the outbreak is focusing around one of them will be automatically implying that this individual is somehow disturbed, "evil," or in some way directly responsible for the disruption. (This implication will be even more profound if you start giving the focal agent all sorts of psychological and neurophysiological tests.) Please remember that a poltergeist-ridden family will sometimes be of low educational status. Often they will not even be capable of understanding the nature of their problem no matter how diligently you might try explaining it to them. By isolating a focal agent, you are telling the family something like, "Well, here's the culprit; here's the person who's to blame for the whole mess." I can well remember how, during one of my own investigations, several family members turned viciously on the likely focal person once I had pointed out how the events seemed to focus on her. The girl was already emotional disturbed, but now became the family scapegoat. She was persecuted by her relatives for causing the disturbances . . . even though I tried to convince them that she was not *consciously* responsible for the disruptions. Isolating a focal agent in this case served merely to intensify stresses and hostilities within the family.

My approach to the study of focal agency has changed as the result of such experiences. When counseling a poltergeist-ridden family, I try to explain that these events are *family* problems. I do not bring forth the likelihood of focal agency unless the family itself has already made this discovery. If I do suspect that a focal agent is present, I usually will give the *entire* family psychological tests as a camouflage to gather the necessary data on the one individual suspected.

SOME FINAL CONSIDERATIONS

Most families bedeviled by poltergeists want the phenomena to cease. They therefore expect the researcher to have the power or knowledge to stop the disturbances, so the ethical investigator must include some counseling specifically addressed to this issue. Because of this problem, I always explain at the very onset of my investigation that parapsychology knows no way to cure such outbreaks. (I even usually warn the families against consulting anyone claiming the power to do so.) Despite this state of affairs, you will very definitely be in a position to advise the family about several courses of action they may take. There is some evidence that religious rites, whether through placebo effect or actual efficacy, do cause some outbreaks to abate. If the family with whom you are dealing is religiously oriented and seems amenable to such a strategy, advising such a course of action entails no breach of conscience. Another way you can deal with this problem is to show the family members how they can actually investigate the poltergeist themselves. Since we have no sure-fire way of curing hauntings and poltergeists, probably the best thing a field investigator can do is turn the family's fear of the unknown into a fascination with it. I have seen very frightened families begin to take great delight and satisfaction in attempting to study what they are up against. With their initial fear conquered, they don't feel inclined to flee from it. This fear can be overcome through proper education and counseling. I can recall one frightened couple who eventually became so fascinated with their poltergeist that they told me how sad they were when it eventually did go away!

On the other hand, if it is clear that the family is dysfunctional or that the dysfunction has led to the outbreak, I feel that the investigator has an ethical responsibility to advise the family to explore family counseling as a likely means of ending the outbreak.

SUMMING UP

Parapsychological field investigators always have a dual responsibility while investigating cases. They have certain obvious professional responsibilities, but they also have the job of helping the families they meet in a humane and sensitive manner. I have learned that sometimes the needs of the family involved will be more pressing than the needs of the investigator. And in these cases, the needs of the family must come first. Sometimes the investigator must take on the role of investigator, social worker, and psychotherapist at one and the same time.

Perhaps I can best summarize this chapter by invoking a principle long revered in clinical psychology. This unwritten law says that the therapist's chief responsibility is to at least leave his clients better off than how he found them. I believe this same principle holds true for you, too, as you seek to confront the poltergeist.

Part 3

Appendixes

Appendix *I*
Epilepsy and the Poltergeist: A historical note

Theories about the nature of poltergeist outbreaks seem to come and go somewhat like fashions in clothing and architecture. Our view about the nature of the poltergeist is once again in flux, due primarily to the recent writings and theories of W. G. Roll of the Psychical Research Foundation, who is currently arguing that such displays might be linked to dysfunctions in the agent's central nervous system. This would suggest that poltergeist outbreaks are neurological as well as psychological phenomena. Roll first developed this theory after investigating a case in which the focal agent suffered grand mal epilepsy, and he has subsequently unearthed evidence that neurological problems may have been complicating factors in some of his earlier cases. Some prodigious historical research undertaken by Mr. Roll also unearthed evidence that symptoms of CNS dysfunction featured prominently in several cases in the literature.

While Roll has certainly done more than any other researcher to focus attention on the physiological and medical aspects of the poltergeist agent, his views and observations are not truly unique. The object of this appendix is to show that Roll's CNS theory is expressing an idea with deep historical roots.

The first presentation of something akin to a CNS theory was actually proposed over thirty years ago by Nandor Fodor, whom we traditionally associate with psychoanalytically derived theories about the poltergeist. It was Fodor who on the basis of his own field investigations first proposed that a poltergeist is a "bundle of projected repressions." Fodor, while conducting research on poltergeists in England, was impressed by two obscure cases he learned about in which direct links between the poltergeist and CNS disturbances existed. The first of these cases (unreferenced by Fodor) involved two soldiers under treatment at Station Hospital in Guernsey. Inexplicable knockings were heard in their presence for ten days. It is interesting that sphygmographic tracings were made of the noises. The doctors treating the patients felt that these poundings were "nervous explosions" somehow linked to chorea, a disease of the central nervous system typified by jerking and other involuntary movements. It is not clear from Fodor's summary, however, whether this condition was formally diagnosed in the case under discussion. What so intrigued Fodor was that the poundings ebbed as the soldiers recovered after being treated with potassium iodide, sodium salicylate, and arsenic. (This was the standard treatment for chorea at the time.) One of the patients had suffered from epilepsy (type unidentified) five years before the current outbreak.

The second case cited by Fodor was drawn from a book written by a British dentist in 1912. E. Howard Grey reported in his book *Visions, Previsions and Miracles* how his own choreic daughter became a poltergeist agent. The outbreak first erupted while he was working on her teeth! The dentist reports about the case:

> We were usually well prepared for these nocturnal troubles by explosive and other auditory sounds, either on the wall or . . . as indeterminate or aerial. Sometimes a tinkling sound as of dropping water would be heard, but none was visible. My wife, a surgeon dentist in active practice for many years, who had also completed a medical curriculum at the University of Boston, and at a London school for women, assisted me in my endeavor to find a natural

cause for these sounds, but without results. She joins me in
affirming that they occurred when the child was asleep, also
in her absence, for instance when she was in bed upstairs we
have heard them in a room below; sometimes her mother
heard them sounding like little taps on a newspaper she
might at the time be reading, and has drawn my attention to
the same.

While Fodor pointed out a link between RSPK and CNS disturbances, he did not champion the theory. He felt that these provocative cases were incipient poltergeists only, but he implied in his
writings that medical factors were perhaps a complicating or
predisposing factor in the etiology of the poltergeist. It is unfortunate that, having pointed out a link between the poltergeist and
CNS disturbances, Fodor never followed up on this lead by com-
menting on it more meaningfully or developing the idea further.
It would appear from his writings that he presented this data only
to prove that the poltergeist was a psychological/psychobiologi-
cal phenomenon and not truly a "supernatural" one. In this
respect, he also cited a case of a woman suffering from hyperthyroidism who also became a poltergeist agent. Although Fodor
preferred to believe that this case had a psychogenic basis, he did
not realize that hyperthyroidism itself can result from psychological factors that eventually disrupt the biochemistry of the body
and brain.* If one can bypass Fodor's incessant and rather arbi-
trary psychoanalytic speculations about the cause of the outbreak, it seems clear that this poltergeist could have resulted
from psychological factors that gave rise to *both* medical and
poltergeist problems.

This is an important possibility, since it potentially serves
as a viable countertheory to Roll's view that poltergeists are, in
some cases, direct projections of CNS disturbances. Perhaps the
severe psychological tensions that appear to lie at the root of
some outbreaks give rise to *both* poltergeist activity and CNS

---

*For a description of the probable biochemistry of this process, refer to Michael
Treisman, "Mind, Body and Behavior: Control Systems and Their Disturbances,"
in *Foundations of Abnormal Psychology*, eds. Perry London and David Rosenhan (New
York: Holt, Rinehart and Winston, 1968).

disturbances. In a case that I personally investigated (refer to Chapter 5), recall that the provisionally identified poltergeist agent only began suffering a temporal lobe symptom *after* the poltergeist had been long active. In this case it looks more as if the neural disruption resulted from the poltergeist rather than precipitated it.

Obviously, much more needs to be done by way of researching the relationship between the poltergeist and CNS disturbances. Researchers have been complacently accepting psychodynamic theories about the poltergeist for some years without seeking to critically evaluate them. This tendency has only now begun to change. So while these widely adopted psychodynamic models have much to teach us, perhaps we should be considering them explanatory *tools* rather than ends in themselves.

This appendix is meant only to show that medical and neurological models for the poltergeist date back many decades, were actually proposed (though only incidentally and provisionally) in 1948, and are certainly not new. The fact that these medical models have survived for so many years certainly suggests that we should be studying them seriously and with an open mind. Perhaps research on the poltergeist will eventually prove what psychology has long realized—that it is virtually impossible to isolate psychological from physiological factors when dealing with human behavior.

Appendix *II*
*Some Further Out-of-Body Poltergeists**

Some thirty years ago, the eminent Hungarian-born psychoanalyst Nandor Fodor suggested that poltergeists might be due to what he called a "psychic lobotomy," which tears loose part of the agent's mental system. He went on to suggest that this system might "float freely" somewhat "like a disembodied entity, but still capable of personality development, as any autonomous complex would be."

Fodor came to this conclusion after making an in-depth study of a poltergeist reported from the early nineteenth century.

I think we should be taking this idea quite seriously. Many current writers on the poltergeist have been openly questioning the theory that RSPK activity can be explained solely as the result of telekinetic activity simply projected by the agent's mind and body. This concept cannot explain the more complex displays of the poltergeist—the production of voices, intelligent and some-

---

*This appendix is expanded from a report delivered at a round table convened at the 1982 convention of the Parapsychological Association held in Cambridge, England.

times veridical communications received from the poltergeist "intelligence" through raps, the appearance of apparitions, the willful and slow-motion carrying of objects from one place to another, the production of specific and complex telekinetic acts at the demand of the witnesses, and others. It often seems that the poltergeist is an agency somewhat distinct from the mind of the agent around whom the events focus, but which is at the same time symbiotically linked to the agent.

This was the basic idea Fodor was getting at, though he never sought to collect specific evidence that could corroborate this theory. Today, thirty years later, we are in a better position, since the study of both the poltergeist and the out-of-body experience (OBE) have come to the forefront of parapsychology. The OBE represents—in my opinion—just such a "tearing loose" of some aspect of the human mind so that it can function independently of the brain and human body. This, of course, leads one to wonder whether there is any sort of inherent connection between the OBE or "bilocation" and the poltergeist. This issue was first raised by Raymond Bayless in 1967 in his book *The Enigma of the Poltergeist,* although he never attempted to collect any empirical evidence that poltergeist displays may somehow be linked to the former phenomenon. This possibility was certainly confirmed by the results of my own exploits recounted in Chapter 8. Further evidence of just this sort can be found by studying the rich historical archives of poltergeist research.

A rather vicious poltergeist attacked a Neapolitan monastery in May 1696 and continued its antics until March 1697. It was eventually written up by Francesco Zingaropoli in his *Gesta di uno spirito nel monastero dei P.P. Gerolomini in Napoli* (1904) and which has recently been rediscovered by Alan Gauld and A. D. Cornell, who discuss it in their book *Poltergeists.* The case included stone-throwings, the production of human yet disembodied voices, the movement of furniture, raps, earthquake-like rumblings, and excrement freely hurled about. The events focused around a young novice named Carlo Maria Valcano, who was having conflicts over his decision to enter monastic life. When he gave up his plans for a religious vocation, the poltergeist ended. However, the most fascinating aspect of the case was that an apparition resembling Carlo was seen in the monastery during the period of the case. The apparition was seen while the novice was at Mass. Since some of the witnesses to these apparitional appearances were relatives of the young man, misidentification seems unlikely. The other residents of the monastery merely assumed that the figure was that of a demon who had taken on Valcano's appearance.

Now let's move ahead a century and a half. In 1860 a poltergeist broke loose in the Swiss home of a lawyer and journalist named Melchior Joller, who wrote an account of the case in a pamphlet *Darstellung selbsterlebter mystischer Erscheinungen.* The episode involved a vast network of paranormal effects, which included the movement of furniture, shadowy apparitions, stonethrowings, apports, and a wide assortment of mysterious sounds. At the height of the case Joller's daughter saw an apparition leaning out of the window of an upper-story room. The figure so resembled a servant girl currently living in the house that the witness called out her name. The servant emerged from the cellar in answer, and at the same time the mysterious apparition dissolved and disappeared. The following extract from Joller's detailed chronology describes the incident:

> About noon, my eldest daughter Emaline was in the garden in bright sunlight. Suddenly hearing a rustling sound in the trellis above, she looked up and saw the figure of a woman leaning out of the window near the little corridor and reaching up to the trellis. Convinced that it was the servant girl coveting grapes, she watched her without exactly being afraid, and it struck her that contrary to her custom she had her hair smoothly parted, wore a hair-net and a dark neck-cloth, and bowed her head in such a melancholy manner. She boldly called the servant girl's name, and the latter emerged from the cellar, whilst the figure vanished as if ducking under the leaves. Thorough investigation revealed nothing more.

The identification of the figure is left a little ambiguous, since Joller does not explain whether his daughter actually *recognized* the figure or merely *assumed* that it was the servant. But the account implies that the daughter was close enough to the trellis where the apparition appeared to make a positive identification. She apparently watched the figure for some time. The fact that it vanished at the time the servant girl physically appeared on the scene also suggests that some relationship existed between the girl and the apparition. The figure was eventually seen on four occasions by five witnesses.

Only a few decades later a similar case struck in England. Brook House in London became the scene of a recalcitrant poltergeist in the late 1880s. The chief witness was Ralph Hastings, who was engaged to the daughter of the residents. He kept detailed notes on the incidents and eventually turned them over to W. T. Stead, the celebrated journalist and social reformer, who published them in the New Year's issue of his magazine *Review of Reviews* in 1892.

The case was fairly typical. Household bells repeatedly rang by themselves, windows opened and closed mysteriously, and thunderous poundings and explosions constantly unnerved the residents. Apparitions were seen on several occasions, and one of them closely resembled Hastings' fiancée. He saw it on more than one occasion.

"As I approached the house from Church Lane," he writes of one of his visits, "I happened to glance at the window to the right on the second floor. There I saw to my astonishment the apparent figure of [my fiancée] standing partially dressed, arranging her hair and looking intently at me." Yet when he entered the house, Hastings found that the young woman was in another part of the house and hadn't stirred from there for quite some time. On another visit both Hastings *and* his fiancée saw the apparition at the same time. They were in the garden when they saw the apparition at a second-story window. It looked just like the young woman but appeared savage and wild. The resemblance was so great that Hastings' fiancée fainted at the sight of it. The phantom gradually disappeared until only its hands remained visible, which closed the window.

Nor must we rely solely on older accounts to find such cases. Nandor Fodor himself noted a similar phenomenon during his investigation of the famous Thornton Heath poltergeist of 1938, which he undertook as director of research for the International

Institute for Psychical Research. This poltergeist was predominantly an object thrower and revolved around a neurotic and sexually disturbed housewife he called Mrs. Forbes in his published accounts on the case. (Her real name was Mrs. Fielding.) On more than one occasion Fodor noted that Mr. Fielding reported seeing his wife at home with him when she was actually out with the investigator himself!

During the height of the case, in fact, Mrs. Forbes started having bilocations, of which some were apparently veridical, as Fodor himself was able to verify. One of these incidents occurred about a month after he entered the case. As Fodor reports:

> Four days later, on March 29th, there was a further development. In the evening she went to the local cinema at Thornton Heath, alone. The film was *The Man Who Lost Himself.* At about 9:00 P.M. she found that she was no longer looking at the screen but was outside Walton House, the headquarters of the International Institute (a distance of ten miles from Thornton Heath), walking up and down opposite the house. At the police station beyond the house she wanted to cross the road, but each time she put her foot on the curb something held her back. She noticed a large car and a blue sedan standing in the mews, and a uniformed chauffeur walking up and down the pavement, following her with his eyes. She noted that Dr. Wills's car was not there, which surprised her, since she knew that a meeting was taking place at which Dr. Wills was supposed to be present. She walked down to Ovington Gardens, crossed Walton Street and looked back towards Walton House. Then she found herself back in the cinema. About a quarter of an hour had passed.

> The description of the cars was not quite correct, but the absence of Dr. Wills's car was a bull's eye. It developed engine trouble at Putney Bridge as he was returning from Thornton Heath. Mrs. Forbes knew nothing of this breakdown and should have expected him to be at the meeting, with the car outside. I found the uniformed chauffeur. He admitted that he walked up and down and saw a young lady with very dark hair and a little round hat, whom he took to be Spanish, staring at him so intently that he began to won-

der what it was about. His description agreed with Mrs. Forbes's appearance and her movements. I asked the chauffeur to call at the Institute and, two days later, placed him behind the door through which Mrs. Forbes was expected to enter into the library. He identified her. Mrs. Forbes, on seeing him, seemed to be struck and searching in her mind. I walked to the chauffeur and whispered to him to put his cap on. As he did so, Mrs. Forbes instantly recognized him.

The weakness of the case resides, of course, in the fact that no one could verify that Mrs. Forbes had indeed been at the theater as she claimed. Fodor himself suggested that she may have undergone a fugue during which she went to Walton House and later regained her memory back at the cinema. This explanation, though viable, cannot explain other instances in which Mrs. Forbes's out-of-body self was seen at some distant location at the very time she was undergoing tests with Fodor at his own institute. Nor would it explain the *errors* Mrs. Forbes made when describing the cars in the above account. This case is unusual since the apparition was not seen actually producing any poltergeist effects, but the fact that Mrs. Forbes (apparently) underwent these experiences and was also the focus of a poltergeist is too coincidental to ignore. It should be noted, however, that Fodor himself never became convinced of the authenticity of Mrs. Forbes's bilocations. He tried to account for these appearances normally, though his explanations (to my mind) seem very labored.

I ran into a similar case in 1973 during my investigation of a poltergeist attacking a middle-class home in a Los Angeles suburb. This was the Carter's family poltergeist that I briefly summarized in Chapter 7. The family was reporting object-movements and other telltale signs of poltergeist infestation, including the odd behavior of a radio that would turn itself on and off and would mysteriously increase volume. On meeting with the family it soon was apparent that they were extremely frustrated over their inability to move from Los Angeles to South America. When they were shown ways of more efficaciously expressing their frustration, the poltergeist ceased. Curiously, an apparition was seen by one of the younger children during the active phase of the case. One night while he was in bed, the child looked up to see the figure of his father in the room with him. The boy merely assumed it *was* his father until the figure dissolved. The child was adamant when I spoke with him about his impression that the figure looked like his father. He maintained that his association of the figure with his father was not merely an assumption he had made.

These cases read so consistently, though separated by both geography and time, that they cannot be simply ignored. They all point in a similar direction—that whatever the nature of the poltergeist, the intelligence guiding these disturbances does not always reside within the brain and body of the agent giving it birth. Some of the more complex and intelligent activities of the poltergeist may result when some aspect of the agent's mind actually becomes independent of the psyche and physically detaches itself—OBE-like—from his/her body. This "free floating" aspect of the agent's mind might thereupon gradually develop a will, intelligence, and personality of its own. It could conceivably build up an apparitional representation of itself, which would resemble the agent; "speak" or otherwise communicate intelligently; carry objects from one room to another; and produce other complex displays. I am not suggesting that this theory accounts for all poltergeists, nor that it need be invoked to explain some of the simpler object-throwing effects that have been studied by myself and other parapsychologists. Cases of disembodied, bilocative, or "lobotomized" poltergeists are probably more rare. However, the peculiar link between poltergeist activity and apparitions of the living suggests that more complex cases may have more complex causes.

I might note by way of conclusion that the theory about complex poltergeist behavior I have been suggesting in this appendix is hardly new. It was perhaps first proposed in 1901 by a German researcher, Herr Kaibel, to account for an Italian rapping poltergeist plaguing the Piazza Santa Croce di Gerusalemme. The case was described in a contemporary issue of *Light*, a Spiritualist newspaper of the time. He believed that the phenomena were being produced by the out-of-body "double" of an invalid woman who was living there. He may well have been right.

REFERENCES

The cases presented in this book have been based on or expanded from technical reports that have appeared in the professional literature. For those readers who want additional or more technical information, the following sources will be of value:

Chapter 1.

A complete report on the Seaford, Long Island poltergeist will be found in W.G. Roll's *The Poltergeist* (New York: New American Library, 1972). The Bridgeport case has never been reported in the professional literature, but a recap of the case plus quotes from the eyewitnesses appears in Dan Greenberg's *Something's There* (Garden City, N.Y.: Doubleday, 1976). The material on the Columbus case is partly drawn from a round table discussion of the case summarized in *Research in Parapsychology—1984* (Metuchen, N.J.: Scarecrow Press, 1985). Articles and interviews on the case also appeared in the September 1984 issue of *Fate* magazine. Some of this information is used here by special permission of the editors. A report on the Miami case by W. G. Roll and J. G. Pratt appeared in the *Journal* of the American Society for Psychical Research, 1971, 15, 409–54. Dr. Bender described his own poltergeist research in the *Proceedings of the Parapsychological Association* #6 published by the P.A. A report on Roll's Michigan case (written with G.F. Solfvin) appeared in *Research in Parapsychology—1975* (*op.cit*, 1976).

Chapter 2.

"A Poltergeist in Los Angeles" is my first detailed account of this challenging case. A brief description of it with an emphasis on the psychodynamics underlying it appeared in *Theta*, 1980, 8 (4), 6–9.

Chapter 3

The chapter on the Simi Valley poltergeist was drawn from an article that appeared in the August 1979 issue of *Fate* magazine. It is reprinted by permission of the editors.

Chapter 4

Raymond Bayless presented his own report on this case in *Theta*, 1980, 8 (3), 9–11.

Chapter 5

My report on the Tucson stone-throwing poltergeist is expanded from a two-part article that appeared in *Fate* magazine, in their November and December 1984 issues. It is used by permission. My technical report is currently pending publication.

Chapter 6

The Rose case of the "odoriferous" poltergeist is reported here for the first time. Both of the other cases in this chapter are more fully discussed in my earlier book *In Search of the Unknown* (New York: Taplinger, 1977).

Chapter 7

A brief report on the Dells' family poltergeist appeared in *Research in Parapsychology—1978* (*op. cit*, 1979). My fuller technical report appeared in the *Journal* of the Society for Psychical Research, 1982, 51, 233–7. My professional report on the briefly mentioned Carter case, with special emphasis on how the case was "cured", was published in the *Journal* of the Society for Psychical Research, 1974, 47, 433–47.

Chapter 8

A more complete analysis of my "out-of-body" haunting appeared in *Theta*, 1978, 6 (2 and 3), 15–20.

Chapter 9

Papers critical of the "repressed hostility" model by Alfonso Martinez Taboas and Carlos S. Alvarado have appeared in the *Parapsychology Review* 1980, 11 (2), 24–27; in the *European Journal of Parapsychology*, 1981, 4, 97–110; and in the *Journal* of the American Society for Psychical Research, 1984, 78, 55–69. My response to these criticisms appeared in the *European Journal of Parapsychology*, 1982, 4, 280–82. The debate between Mr. Martinez Taboas and myself over the Dell case appeared in the *Journal* of the Society for Psychical Research, 1982, 51, 401–3 and 1983, 52, 154–5. W.G. Roll's full explication of the epilepsy/poltergeist connection appeared in the *European Journal of Parapsychology*, 1978, 2, 167–200. Mr. Martinez Taboas' reply is contained in the *Journal* of the American Society for Psychical Research paper cited above.

BIBLIOGRAPHY

Bayless, Raymond. *The Enigma of the Poltergeist.* (West Nyack, New York: Parker, 1967.)

Carrington, Hereward and Fodor, Nandor. *Haunted People—The Story of the Poltergeist Down Through the Centuries.* (New York: Dutton, 1951.)

Fodor, Nandor. *On the Trail of the Poltergeist.* (New York: Citadel, 1958.)

Gauld, Alan and Cornell, A. D. *Poltergeists.* (London: Routledge and Kegan Paul, 1979.)

Goss, Michael. *Poltergeists: An Annotated Bibliography of Works in English, Circa 1880–1975.* (Metuchen, New Jersey: Scarecrow Press, 1979.)

Owen, A. R. G. *Can We Explain the Poltergeist?* (New York: Garrett, 1964.)

Rogo, D. Scott. *An Experience of Phantoms.* (New York: Taplinger, 1974.)

———. *The Poltergeist Experience.* (New York: Penguin, 1979.)

Roll, W. G. *The Poltergeist.* (New York: New American Library, 1972.)

INDEX

Printed in May 2021
by Rotomail Italia S.p.A., Vignate (MI) - Italy